Confessions
of a
Pilgrim

Andrea.
Enjoy the journey!

Sue Kenny
2009

Journeys of Discovery

When I launched BookShorts, I knew it would be an arduous journey. Book publishing is a quirky business, full of brilliant people and at the same time, rife with the realities of those very people working hard to justify every entrepreneurial initiative in the context of slim margins and limited resources. Meeting Sue Kenney at a pivotal moment in the company's evolution, reading her work, striving to help her reach her audience through the medium of moving pictures, re-invigorated my own commitment. Her dedication has given me invaluable perspective about persevering, about how to reach one's goals. Her story continues to inspire me and Book-Shorts, every day.

Judith Keenan
Founder/Executive Producer
BookShorts Literacy Program
www.BookShorts.com

**Other Books
Sue Kenney's
My Camino
Published by White Knight Books
Toronto, Canada**

The true story of the spiritual quest of a woman confronting her deepest fear.

ISBN 09734186-3-X

An incredible story of courage.
Robert Crew, Travel Editor Toronto Star

Heartfelt and authentic, My Camino gives us the courage to get off the treadmill of contemporary life and experience the creative and spiritual release of simple walking. Anita Shuper, Toronto, Ontario

You have inspired me to shift some sort of internal paradigm, which I am unable to articulate at this time. All I would like to say is, I enjoyed your book, your movie and your One Woman Show in London. You are a strong and powerful woman of integrity and depth.
Candace Lawrence,
Kings College University, London, Ontario

Confessions of a Pilgrim

by Sue Kenney
Author of *My Camino*

Edited by Bruce Pirrie

iUniverse, Inc.
New York Lincoln Shanghai

Confessions of a Pilgrim

iUniverse books may be ordered through booksellers or by contacting:

iUniverse
2021 Pine Lake Road, Suite 100
Lincoln, NE 68512
www.iuniverse.com
1-800-Authors (1-800-288-4677)

The views expressed in this work are solely those of the author and do not necessarily reflect the views of the publisher, and the publisher hereby disclaims any responsibility for them.

Editor Bruce Pirrie
Copy Edit by Rick Book
Cover design by Robert Keenan
Cover photo courtesy of Pasha Patriki

ISBN: 978-0-595-42790-1 (pbk)
ISBN: 978-0-595-87122-3 (ebk)

Printed in the United States of America

For Mum

Contents

Foreword

Dreams have always figured prominently in the lives of First Nation people. The messages that come to us through our dreams come directly from the spirit world. Many people today choose to ignore these messages sent to them in the dark. I was taught to pay attention to them as I come from a long line of dreamers. I knew before Sue left for her pilgrimage on the Camino that I had to tell her of my dream vision about her journey. I didn't know whether or not Sue would find the next carrier of the Eagle Feather on her trip. It wasn't for me to figure out.

It would take a lifetime to pass on all the teachings of the Eagle Feather. I can only share a minuscule part of them here. An Eagle Feather does not belong to the person who carries it. They never own it; they will only carry it for a little while. The Eagle Feather is destined to go somewhere else to continue its work. It must be cared for. It is a living being and is to be treated with respect at all times. The Eagle Feather that came to me from Alberta was sent to Spain with Sue, as it was meant to be. Sue was sent to send it on with someone else to continue its teaching journey somewhere else on Mother Earth.

One underlying theme comes out in everything my elders have taught me—the Creator's hand guides each of us. Again, whether we choose to believe it or not, we need to have faith. We need to be open to the possibilities, watch for the signs and listen to the messages sent to us in our dreams.

I am grateful for the many gifts I have been given. I am honoured to be a small part of this important story during the time of the Seventh Fire. I believe that Creation is unfolding exactly as it should.

Sherry Lawson
Mnjikaning First Nation
January 2007

Map of the Camino Routes

Courtesy of Tourist Office of Spain—Canada

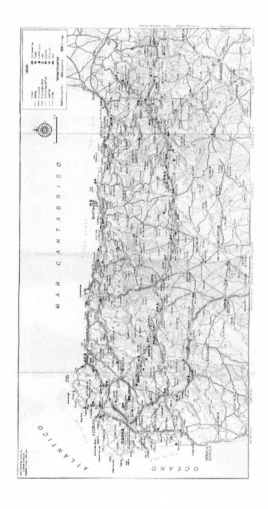

The Road to Santiago

Written by Mony Dojeiji

The Camino de Santiago de Compostela is a series of 1100 year old European pilgrimage routes that converge in Santiago, Spain. Camino means *the way*. To tread the ancient route is to walk in the footsteps of hope, faith and trust. Pilgrims walk thousands of kilometres to venerate the remains of Saint James the Apostle, which are allegedly buried in the Cathedral there. They believe that if they are close to the remains of an Apostle, they are closer to God.

Celtic in origin, Catholic by conquest, the Camino today calls modern seekers to walk along its well-worn paths. From the majestic heights of the Pyrenees Mountains, through the lush wine fields of La Rioja, the arid wheat fields of its Meseta and the sea-side coast of Galicia, the pilgrims walk, bicycle or sometimes even ride a horse.

Travelling in groups or completely alone, they set out on their journey guided by the distinctive yellow arrows and scallop shell signs that show the way to the magnificent eleventh century Cathedral of Santiago. However, following the invisible arrows of the heart is often where one truly experiences the allure of the Camino. Although volumes of written texts can be found, it is in the silence of the way where the pilgrim's answers are heard. In surrendering to the Camino and allowing it to guide, a true inner journey is revealed.

On their journey of self-healing and self-discovery, the pilgrim invariably experiences the infinite love of the Camino.

Mony Dojeiji is a Canadian pilgrim who has walked the Camino Frances. Along with her husband, they completed a pilgrimage from Rome to Jerusalem for peace. They are currently writing their story and can be reached at monydojeiji@hotmail.com.

Preface

In choosing the title *Confessions of a Pilgrim,* I employed the word confession not necessarily in its Roman Catholic context, as an admission of guilt or sin, but rather in reference to its other meaning, as exemplified by Leo Tolstoy in his essay *Confessions,* that of a public declaration or affirmation of beliefs. In doing research for the book I was pleasantly surprised when I unearthed an even older usage of the word, coming from the Latin *confessio,* which was originally used to designate the burial place of the remains of a Saint. This providential discovery, especially in a story about my journey to the tomb of Saint James, filled me with an appreciation for the role of serendipity in our lives.

It is said that you are never alone on the Camino. Through these stories, it is my intention to inspire you in some way. It is also my hope that the Camino stories will open possibilities for you as you travel on your life journey. May you have the comfort of knowing that you are never alone.

Buen Camino.
Sue Kenney

Acknowledgments

My gratitude goes to all the women in my life, especially my precious daughters Tara, Meghan and Simone. To my Mum, and to my Dad. To all of my sisters, my brother and their families: Patricia and John Harber, the late Donna Graham, Kevin Graham, Lori and Dave Bos, Joanne and Doug Scott, Larry and Joanne Regan, Kelly and Rob Gibbs, and to Darrell and Aaron. Special thanks to my nieces and nephews too. To my Grandmothers, who taught me about the virtue of serving. To John Kenney and his family for being a special part of my life.

Thanks to all of my girlfriends especially Luba Paolucci, Mony Dojeiji and Audrey Smith. To Brenda Baird for creating my website and Judith Keenan for making movies about books. To Brigitte, the Austrian pilgrim and all my grade-school teachers who said I was too talkative. Special thanks to Linda, at the Longford Post Office.

Eternal thanks to Andreas Laus for sharing the Sorrow Stone story. To Acacio da Paz for his guidance. Wende Bartley for sharing your voice and your studio and Bob Derkach for the Camino *tunage*. Thank you to Maggie, Audrey, Suzie, Janet, Mark, Erin, Faith, Sharon and Anna for being great leaders. Special thanks to my cottage neighbours in Floral Park, especially Eleanor and to the Elders in Washago. Thanks to Greg Morrison and Sandra Balcovske for sharing your home and to the artists at the Gibraltar Point Centre for the Arts for their inspiration. To my friends at DARE for their healing. I'm forever grateful to my rowing crews and especially my coaches Paul Westbury and Peter Cookson for the life lessons. Thanks to Rick Book for becoming a part of this journey at the perfect time. To the pilgrims I met on my journey especially Judith, Nathalie, Lynn, Rosemary, Carlos, Janine, Maria, Alberto, Santiago and Marius.

With all my love and humble gratitude, I thank Bruce Pirrie. Both your editing talent and tenacity has kept me on my path. I am truly grateful for your humour, unconditional love and for the extraordinary contribution you've made to my life. A big thanks to Laurel for your help and patience while we worked on the book.

To my publisher Bill Belfontaine, White Knight Books for being there from the very beginning. Thanks to Pierre Even at Cirrus Productions for your dedication to sharing my story. To all the pilgrim associations, Tourism Spain, Tour Galicia, The Spanish Centre, Xunta de Galicia, the volunteers and those who work to keep the Camino alive.

Miigwech to Sherry Lawson. You have bestowed a great honour on me and I will forever be grateful to you. Thank you for trusting and for telling the stories of the First Nation people. I will forever carry the message of the Eagle Feather and you in my soul.

I humbly give thanks and praise to God and the Creator.

Introduction

It's March 10th, 2002. A few days after my forty-sixth birthday, with my sixty-nine year old mother in tow, I embarked on a journey to the Fifth Annual American Pilgrim Gathering which was being held in Williamsburg, Virginia, that year. We drove from Toronto for eleven hours straight in order to get there. Arriving late, we were quietly ushered into a room that was packed with pilgrims. There was a friendly-looking middle-aged couple were standing up and talking to the group about their recent journey on the Camino de Santiago de Compostela. When they finished, everyone clapped and a woman next to them rose to her feet and began to tell her story. Soon it became obvious that each person in the room was taking a turn to introduce themselves to the group and share a personal anecdote.

Keen to learn more, I listened eagerly as the last few stories were told. Most people spoke with anticipation about planning their next walk on the Camino. I was puzzled by the fact people would want to go back, not once, but three or four times. Although life-changing and spiritually rewarding, my personal pilgrimage had been quite mentally and physically challenging. I wondered what could possibly be driving them to return. Suddenly the room went silent, everyone was looking at me. It was my turn to speak but I hadn't thought about what I was going to say. I took a centering breath, stood up and introduced myself and my Mum.

"My name is Sue Kenney. I'm here with my mother, June Regan, who has not walked the Camino but has been on her own incredible life journey raising seven children." The audience applauded and my Mum waved back. "A few months ago, I returned home after walking from St. Jean Pied de Port to Santiago on the French Route. I did it alone. To complicate things, I don't speak a word of Spanish and I didn't take a map with me." Then I told them I was a single mother with three teenaged daughters.

"Unlike many of you, I have absolutely no desire to walk the Camino again—ever." There was some gentle laughter but also a few expressions of surprise. My heart raced as I continued, feeling very nervous about speaking in front of the group. "When I was suddenly downsized from my twenty-year corporate telecom career, I decided to walk the Camino to gain a clearer understanding of my life purpose." "I feel as though I learned more in twenty-nine days of walking on the Camino than I have throughout most of my adult life. It was like each day on the Camino was the equivalent of one year of my life." Pausing to take a breath, I looked more closely at the people in the room and remembered that they were pilgrims just like me. My nervousness dissolved and suddenly I felt completely at home with these fellow travellers.

"Right now, I'm sure it'll take me another lifetime to distill and integrate all that I've learned on my Camino journey." They applauded. I quickly sat down beside Mum, relieved that I'd spoken those words out loud because it confirmed how I honestly felt.

Several months after attending the Gathering, I left Toronto, where I had lived all my life and moved into my ninety-five year old clapboard cottage in a small village on a lake in Ramara Township. I longed to be close to nature all the time. It was two hours north of the city and far away from the noise and pollution of Toronto's two and a half million people. After walking the Camino, I had struggled to integrate the virtues of being a simple pilgrim into my life when I returned to the world back home. Finding a job that offered monetary bonuses, extra vacation, benefits and perks didn't resonate with me anymore. A look around my home told me I had acquired too much already. I made the conscious decision to live the virtues of a pilgrim, giving away most of my belongings and moving up north. For the first time, I felt I was being an active leader in my own life by choosing to create a path to contribute something special to the universe based on the gifts I had been given.

Within months of moving to my cottage, an opportunity came up to take over a village gift store called The Whistle Stop located nearby in the town of Washago. Strangely, I had this nagging sense that someone was trying to find me and they couldn't. I didn't know who they were or why they wanted to reach me. I just had a feeling I couldn't explain. Against all of my logical business instincts, I took over the seasonal retail business.

Before I knew it, I was relaying the history of the Camino and tales of my life-altering journey to the people who came into the store and anyone else who'd listen. I talked about how the encounters with pilgrims I'd met from all over the world had provided insights into my own inner journey.

As my storytelling skills improved, I shared even more intimate details of my inner quest. People were intrigued and I was absolutely convinced they wanted to hear more. Often I was reminded of Brigitte, an Austrian pilgrim whom I had met when I walked the Camino in the winter of 2001. One day during a conversation over breakfast, she had suggested I should be a storyteller. She'd said that I had a strong voice and that people would listen to me. After assuring her that all of my life I'd been told that I talked too much she still insisted. "Go and speak." Brigitte's words that day helped me to realize that my voice was a gift that I could use to fulfill my life purpose to inspire others. It was distressing to think that I'd spent most of my life and a lot of energy suppressing one of my most precious natural talents. Years ago—it seemed like a lark at the time—I had kissed the Blarney Stone in Ireland. As the folklore suggested, maybe it had bestowed upon me the storytelling gift of my Irish ancestors.

Using my speaking voice to tell stories of the Camino was the only way I knew how to manifest my life purpose. I even recorded and produced a storytelling CD. People loved listening to the stories and the feedback was rewarding. Many people wanted me to write a book. I resisted. In my mind I wasn't a writer. One day, about a year later, I woke up with a very slight but insightful shift in my perspective. For the first time, I could see that the stories from the Camino weren't just about me; they were simple yet profound tales of a journey that I believed were given to me as a gift. Therefore, it didn't matter whether I thought I was a writer or not because I knew for certain that I had an obligation to share these stories with others. If I didn't, I would be doing a disservice to the Camino and to myself. There was no way for me to know who would be affected by them, or how the Camino might inspire others on their own life journey. With this intention in mind, I believed that I could attract from the universe whatever was required for me to write a book and at the same time, give something back to the Camino.

1

An Editor Appears

In the fall of 2003, the universe provided. *Word on the Street* is a popular literary festival in Toronto. For one day in September, Queen Street West is blocked off and thousands of booklovers from seniors to children descend on the open-air market of books, author readings and booths set up by publishing houses, distributors and writing associations. It's the modern version of a medieval market, but instead of vegetables, animals and alchemists, there are piles and displays of all kinds of books.

Although I hadn't actually written anything yet, I decided to go to the festival to see if I could find a publisher. I left early in the morning armed with a handful of my Stone by Stone storytelling CDs, a stack of flyers and an idea for a book. After a few hours of walking around I approached a booth where a friendly gray haired man was standing. He invited me over and I introduced myself as a storyteller. I told him about my idea to write a book on the Camino. His name was Bill Belfontaine and he was very interested in my story. He was also the publisher of White Knight Books.

Excitedly, I showed him my CD and explained how people had responded favourably to my stories. He handed me his business card and I filed it in the back pocket of my jeans, separating it from the other contacts I had made that day. When he asked me to provide him with a sample of my writing, I knew a possibility had been opened. I assured him that I would have an outline, marketing plan and a sample of my writing to him within the next two weeks. Thanking him profusely, I turned and walked away wondering just how I was going to pull this off.

I delivered on my promise and Bill was pleased with the writing sample and the marketing package. He agreed to publish my book for release the following summer; a very short timeline. In order to do this I had to get a draft manuscript to him in two months time. He told me that he'd need at least 50,000 words since he would only publish a book that was two hundred pages or longer. To meet this deadline, I committed myself to writing 1000 words a day for the next sixty days.

Throughout that winter while I wrote, I always had a pot of homemade soup warming on the stove as it kept me going through the long, cold days. I spent a lot of time alone and sometimes worried I would become like the writers I had read about—reclusive, drunks and reprobates basically. But since I don't drink much, except for the occasional glass of red wine and I wasn't about to take up smoking since I had asthma, I felt reasonably safe. Instead, yoga, meditation and a walk everyday fuelled my creativity.

Often I worked on my manuscript when business was slow at The Whistle Stop. I absolutely trusted that if my intentions and actions were true to my life purpose, the right people and situations would be presented. One day Tara, my oldest daughter, came to help me out at the store. Shortly after she arrived, the door opened and a tall attractive woman named Fran and her adorable seven-year-old daughter, Laurel, came in. I'd met them once before at the Farmers Market in Orillia just before Christmas. Laurel went straight to an open suitcase filled with kids' toys and Fran came up to the counter. She invited Tara and I to her annual New Year's Day party at their nearby farm. As they were leaving, I let her know that I would probably be working on my book and not able to make it.

Early in the afternoon on New Year's Day, I was busy working on the book when the phone rang.

"Are you going, Mum?" It was Tara reminding me of Fran's party at the farm. I had completely forgotten about it. "You're not socializing enough. It'll be good for you to get out," she said with my best interest at heart. Since I'd been spending most of my time alone, I felt like I actually needed a break from my work so I decided to go.

Off came the yoga pants, wool sweater and sports bra. I had a quick shower; on went my low-rise jeans, a wide belt, a push-up bra, a black turtleneck sweater and my tan-coloured leather jacket. I topped it all off by putting on black mascara and some lipstick too.

Outside, I brushed the snow off my car and warmed it up. I drove to Fran's, alone again but excited to meet her friends. There were mostly women at the party and Fran introduced me to everyone in the room. I took a seat on the couch and started talking to a man sitting at the other end with his arms crossed tightly. It turned out that he was Fran's ex-husband and Laurel's father. His name was Bruce. We started to talk casually and I found myself studying his mannerisms. Our eyes rarely made contact but when they did, I was drawn in. He had an exceptionally brilliant sense of humour and made me laugh a lot. I found out that Bruce had grown up in Toronto too. We talked about the things we missed about living in the city. He also liked a good cup of espresso coffee and the ethnic restaurants that served more than the local Orillia staples—burgers and beer. Conversation with him was stimulating; a welcome relief from my solitary winter life in a small cottage community.

Suddenly he became very animated and said, "Let's get out of here and go for an espresso!" I laughed at the idea.

"Where would we go?" I asked. "It's New Years Day."

"Oh, I don't know," he said dryly. "How about Toronto?" His eyes sparkled peeking over the rimless glasses that rested lightly on his perfectly-shaped nose. I told him that I really had to get home to finish writing my book, his eyes opened wide. "You're a writer?" I nodded back to him. "I'm a writer too," he said earnestly, "I'd love to read your material if you ever want someone to take a look at it." I immediately thanked him for his generous offer, knowing I wouldn't let just anyone read my work. Besides, I wasn't ready to release my story to the rest of the world yet, let alone a guy I just met at a party. Then, like Cinderella, I jumped up realizing it was time to go. I hadn't spoken to the other people at Fran's party because Bruce had commandeered all of my time, so rather quickly, I got up and made my way around the room.

Just as I was leaving, Bruce said, "I'll walk you to your car." On the way out, he told me he was a writer on the CBC television series called *The Red Green Show*. Even though I didn't watch the show, I knew it was a phenomenally successful Canadian television comedy show about an eccentric yet loveable handyman who uses lots of duct tape. There wasn't a single female character so I was sure Bruce wouldn't be interested in my personal story about a woman's spiritual quest on a medieval pilgrimage route in Spain. It was so cold outside so it didn't take long for him to say good-bye. I drove straight home from the party and thought about Bruce's offer. When I got home I put some soup on the stove and began working on a problematic chapter which I had ironically entitled *Clarity of Vision*.

Over the next few weeks, Bruce came to The Whistle Stop to visit almost every day. We mostly talked about writing and I was especially intrigued by our discussions about the creative process.

One day he asked me, "Have you ever read your work out loud?"

A little confused by his suggestion, I shook my head. "No I haven't. Why are you asking?"

"Well, if you don't read what you've written out loud, then how will you know what it sounds like?"

I was impressed. His words resonated with me. I thought if I was truly living my life purpose, by using my voice to share stories of the Camino, then it made perfect sense for me to hear what I'd written out loud. It was the best editing advice I'd ever heard. That day it occurred to me that maybe I had attracted Bruce to help me fulfill my life purpose. I also questioned whether he was the person who was looking for me.

"Wait here for a minute," I said running to the backroom. Finding the hard copy of my manuscript stored in a cardboard shirt box under the counter, I pulled out one of the chapters. When I returned, I handed Bruce the chapter entitled *Clarity of Vision*. "Here's some of my writing. It's a bit convoluted and my thoughts are totally disorganized. Actually, I can't seem to sort out what I really want to say. If your offer is still there, I'd appreciate your comments." He took the sheets and left saying he was going to start reading right away.

The next morning at 9:00 a.m. the phone rang. It was Bruce calling with an offer.

"I've got some feedback on your writing. If you're interested, I could come over and we could talk about it." I could feel tension building in my neck. My hands went clammy, my throat felt swollen. I was so afraid he was going to tell me that my writing wasn't very good. Before I could say anything he said, "I'll be over in 20 minutes." Now I couldn't say no. I put a pot of espresso coffee on and before it was ready he arrived at the cottage door. We got to work right way. The formerly loose papers were now held together with a black clip on the side of the page. There were comments, arrows and red markings all over the pages.

He said he liked my writing style and gave me some basic writing tips. The one that helped me the most was his suggestion to put like-with-like and link the same ideas together. He offered direct, intense feedback, without judgment of me as a person or a writer.

He didn't change my words, but instead he moved the words around. It took an hour to cover his notes. He had logically and creatively distilled and clarified the chapter and without really thinking too much, I asked him if he would consider editing my book.

"Sure," he said without hesitation. "Have you got the rest of the manuscript here?" Since I was in the habit of carrying the manuscript back and forth to the store, I had a copy to give to him. We finished our espresso and he left saying he wanted to get to work. Days later, he told me that he had never edited a book before. With his years of experience writing, directing and performing, it was clear that he could transfer his skills and natural talent with ease. It didn't seem to matter to Bruce if the material was comedic, spiritual or dramatic, for him the creative process was the same. Part of the secret to his brilliance, I thought, was his ability to see the story from beginning to end like he was watching a movie. Above all, he taught me how to think like a writer.

Editing the book took a couple of months. During this time, we spent many hours together and Bruce admitted that he had fallen in love with me. I told him that I struggled with the notion of being in a romantic relationship since I felt this incredibly strong urge to pursue my life work alone. I knew this book had to be finished outside the confines of a love affair and unhampered by any distractions. I couldn't tell him that there was another fear I had—deep inside—I was afraid I might write a book that would actually inspire people. In fact, I was more afraid of that than I was of failing at writing a book. I knew this was all a part of facing my deepest fear; living my life purpose.

2

A Familiar Calling

As I came closer to completing the manuscript, I felt a familiar calling. It was the strong desire to go for a walk—a very long walk. I yearned to be on the road again living the simple life of a pilgrim. I tried to ignore it, since I had way too much to do. Again and again, I asked myself the same question. "Why I should return to the Camino?" Putting the manuscript for *My Camino* aside I decided to check my calendar, just to see if there was a possibility that I could go. I was surprised to find out that, except for a speaking engagement early in the month, I had nothing booked for the last three weeks of April. I'd been so busy working on the manuscript that I'd neglected to fill my calendar with paying work.

Daydreaming about what it would be like to walk the Camino again, I shuddered at the thought of being in the cold Spanish spring rain and being soaked through to my underwear. Yet, I loved the sense of freedom, the movement of my body, the sun on my face and the wind at my back. I knew intimately the physical and emotional trials of walking twenty to forty kilometres every day carrying ten kilos of weight in my backpack. I was convinced that in order to live my true destiny, I must be outside my comfort zone and on the Camino I would be. Even though it would be my second time walking the Camino, I suspected another pilgrimage could present more challenging life lessons, even possibly the same lessons I thought I'd learned the first time.

Later that day I called my dear friend Andreas in Germany, anxious to tell him about my plans. We had met near the end of my first Camino. As pilgrims we walked together for six days and then fell deeply in love. At the time, he was twenty-nine years old and I was forty-five. After we returned home, we spent a year involved in an intensely passionate long distance love affair. We flew back and forth across the Atlantic to visit on numerous occasions, finding that everything we were looking for in life was fulfilled when we were together.

The last time I had seen Andreas was almost a year before when I went to Berlin for ten days just before Christmas. We had a magical time together. During that visit, Andreas invited me to live with him. I was thrilled and immediately began making plans to move to Germany. It seemed everything in my life had opened up for this next step. My daughters had all moved away from my home and they didn't require my daily presence. At the time, I was building my speaking and coaching practice, but it could be scheduled from anywhere in the world. Andreas had a promising career working for a large consulting firm, and he had a fabulous apartment in Berlin that was big enough for both of us. I could leave the cottage in Canada with all of my personal things safely stored and return to visit my daughters, family and friends at any time.

Everything seemed to be unfolding perfectly yet when I went back home after that visit, I felt unusually sad. I didn't understand why, but something didn't feel right about my decision to move there. Weeks later, I struggled through an emotional roller coaster for a number of days—I thought I was pregnant. I'd decided that if I was, I'd accept the child as a gift from God. Andreas and I talked on the phone about having a child together. He confessed that he really wanted to have a family. I was in my mid-forties and had long ago decided I wasn't having any more children, if it was my choice. A few days later I found out that I wasn't pregnant after all. Having a family together developed into an issue we couldn't resolve. With much regret, I cancelled my plans to move to Germany.

We had remained constantly in touch by e-mail and by phone, but I hadn't seen him in over a year. Even still, I was constantly being drawn to him as though there was something left unfinished in our relationship. On the phone that day, Andreas surprised me when he said he was envious that I was walking the Camino again. He offered to join me. For a moment I seriously considered the idea. As difficult as it was to say no, my intuitive logic told me I must be alone on this journey.

3

Bernie the Dog

Contrary to what I'd proclaimed to the pilgrims at the Gathering in Williamsburg, I was ready to return to the Camino. Working through the stories for my book had reminded me of an encounter with a dog I'd met on my first walk. His name was Bernie and he was a legend on the Camino.

One morning, I arrived in the village of Castro Jerez and stopped for a *cafe con leche* at a local restaurant. When I opened the door, a huge German Shepherd dog ran across the room toward me. Just as he was about to jump up, the owners called out and he stopped. They told me his name was Bernie. He slept at my feet while I ate breakfast, acting like he was my long-lost pet. Later, when I got up to leave with another pilgrim, Stefan the Argentinean, Bernie followed us out the door. He walked with me for the entire day, even after Stefan had walked on ahead.

Six hours later, Bernie and I arrived in Fromistra, a village about twenty-four kilometres from the restaurant. As we came into town, I stopped to admire the sunset and complete the ritual of spending time at the end of each day in a state of gratitude. Bernie waited at my feet. Across the road I heard voices calling out, "*Hola* Bernie. *Hola*!" I wondered how they knew him. We walked together to the albergue. When we got to the pilgrim's hostel, I met Stefan and he told me that Bernie was a legend on the Camino. Each day, he chose a pilgrim to walk with and on that day, he'd picked me. The reason everyone in the village knew Bernie was because he always refused to walk back home again. Someone from the village either had to drive him back home or call his owner to come and pick him up.

While writing the Camino stories, I started to realize that my Camino was a lot like Bernie's. When I reached Santiago, I didn't have to turn around and walk back home like the pilgrims of the past. Instead, as a modern-day pilgrim, I rented a car and drove back, covering the distance in eight hours it had taken me twenty-nine days to walk. Once in Santiago, I boarded a train to Paris, and caught a plane to Toronto where my sister and my daughters were waiting to drive me home, just like Bernie.

My journey, however arduous, was a far cry from those of the pilgrims of the past. They would walk out the front door of their homes, leaving their families behind and join other pilgrims on the path. They didn't have yellow arrows to follow. Their destination was the glorious Cathedral of Santiago where the body of Saint James the Apostle was buried and they walked because they believed if they were closer to the remains of an Apostle, they would be closer to God.

Along the way, many perished from illness, robbery or even starvation. If they were lucky enough to make it to Santiago and take the sacraments of Communion and Confession, they were told they would be absolved from eternal damnation. Following completion of the rituals, they would turn around and begin a new journey—walking the same route back home, fully aware of the dangers they could encounter but perhaps now buoyed by their renewed faith. Knowing this, I made the promise to myself that one day I would return to the Camino and authentically walk the route like the pilgrims of the past. I suspected there would be a lot more for me to learn by retracing my own footsteps. To do this and honour the pilgrims of the past, I decided I would return to walk the less-travelled Portuguese Route following the Galician coast, this time in both directions.

The next morning, Bruce and I were discussing the final editing notes on the manuscript when I announced to him that I was going back to the Camino. I knew it would be difficult for him to accept as our relationship had developed and we'd become very close. He knew all about my commitment to my life work and the whole story of Andreas, from working on the book. I explained to him that the Camino was calling to me but I didn't really understand why.

"Then you have to go," he said.

4

The Journey of an Eagle Feather

A couple of weeks before I was to leave, I started a seven-day grape fast to cleanse my body in preparation for the journey. I sent an e-mail to everyone on my lengthy address list announcing my plans to return to the Camino and offered to take their personal intentions with me to leave in Santiago. Right away, I heard back from my friend, Sherry, who lived on the Chippewas of Mnjikaning First Nation. When I moved up to my cottage in Ramara, she was one of the first local people who befriended me. Her e-mail said that she must see me before I leave. She'd said that she had a vivid dream about me that she must share.

As the daughter of a past Chief and the first Native woman in the area to become a Justice of the Peace, Sherry was highly respected and honoured in the community. We arranged to meet at The Whistle Stop. Sherry arrived, wearing business clothes. Her short brown hair was neatly styled and as always she was in a cheerful mood. Sherry was a great storyteller and we loved to share our personal experiences. That day, I was eager to hear about her dream. Unexpectedly Sherry said she had to get something from the car and rushed out of the store. After a few minutes, which seemed like hours, she came back and presented me with a gift. It was a small flat package wrapped in red cloth with a piece of deerskin tied around it. I looked at her, mystified. She spoke in a calm tone, suggesting I open it. I untied it and folded open the fabric. Inside there was a beautiful light brown coloured feather. I suspected it was an Eagle Feather but I'd never seen one before and I wasn't sure why she was giving it to me. I looked in her shining brown eyes waiting for her to speak.

"In my dream, I was told to give this to you," she explained. She was given a message to send the Eagle Feather with me on my return journey to the Camino. I listened to her words carefully. She spoke slowly in a low-key but authoritative voice. "The red fabric is its home. When you are holding the Eagle Feather, you are in direct contact with the Creator." I knew the Eagle soared above all the other birds and represented wisdom but I wasn't sure why she was giving this great honour to me. I wondered what had I done to deserve this. Emotionally stirred and in a state of shock, I didn't know what to say or how to react. My body became numb. My hands shook as I carefully lifted the feather out of the red fabric and held it gently. With honour and admiration I looked directly at Sherry and then bowed my head.

"Th-thank you," I stammered. "This is a great honour and I am humbled. What am I supposed to do with this Sherry? What does the Eagle Feather have to do with your dream?" I asked.

She nodded, understanding my concerns and then began explaining that in her dream she received a message that I was to take it with me on my long journey. Before returning home, I would give it to someone who was not from the country I was from.

"That person," she said, "will take the Eagle Feather to another country, a place where you are not from. The recipient will carry the Eagle Feather's story and that of the Native People with it on their journey." On hearing the instructions, I became even more nervous about this responsibility. My entire body began trembling uncontrollably so I set the Eagle Feather down. Sherry assured me that as long as I was in possession of the Eagle Feather, it would protect me on my journey. That was a consolation. She was insistent that the Eagle Feather never be exposed to alcohol or any mood-altering drugs.

Sherry was sending me on a mission to find a worthy recipient for the Eagle Feather. She then said the recipient would acknowledge me with kindness, honour and love. As I listened to her, I wasn't sure how on Earth I was going to do this but I knew that if trusted in the Camino, the answers would come to me. On my first pilgrimage, I had gone on a spiritual quest to find self-love and overcome my deepest fear: facing the truth about my life-purpose and how to use the gifts I had been given. I learned that if I asked for a sign, one would be delivered. On this quest, I just wanted to be alone and live the simple life of a pilgrim again. Before taking on the mission to find a recipient for this great honour, I thought, my journey would be easier than the last one.

I couldn't have been more wrong.

5

Leaving the Ordinary World

It isn't uncommon for me to lose things that come into my procession: sunglasses, books, clothes, even money. I was afraid of losing the Eagle Feather so I slipped it into a deerskin wallet I had purchased at a nearby moccasin shop in Ramara. Most of the clothes that I had taken on my first journey were coming with me once again, along with a lighter sleeping bag, a silk liner and a smaller backpack loaned by a friend. I found a small black leather change purse in my dresser drawer, and filled it with my Visa card, bankcard and more than $600.00 cash. Then I took out a little black velvet bag and filled it with a few of my favourite stones to give away to pilgrims I would meet on the way.

Finally, I finished packing and without much time to spare, I tucked the wallet with the Eagle Feather into a deep pocket on the inside of my coat, near my heart. I was confident that it would be safe there. I was driving myself to the airport but I had one stop to make on the way—a funeral home on Dufferin Street in Toronto to pay my respects to a dear friend Pat, who had died just days before. She had died of Multiple Sclerosis after a difficult battle that had lasted more than twenty years.

My sister, Lorie, and her husband, Dave, were standing in the hall outside the funeral home. In a hushed voice, I asked Lorie to hold my hiking jacket while I went inside to where Pat's body was resting. I approached the family to express my condolences. Feeling inadequate in their time of grief, I promised them that I would walk the Camino with Pat's memory in my intentions. I would carry a special stone for her to the Cathedral in Santiago de Compostela and place it near the remains of the Apostle. Then I knelt down by the casket and prayed. It felt odd to be there, facing the darkness of death and despair just as I was embarking on a journey filled with new life and hope.

At the back of the chapel, Lorie handed me my coat. As I was leaving, she called out to me, "Susan, is that yours?" She was pointing to the floor. I looked down, horrified to see my little black wallet stuffed with all the money I had for this journey, along with my bankcard and credit card. Thanking her, I picked it up and shoved it in my coat pocket again. In a panic, I checked to see if I still had the Eagle Feather. Thank God, it was there.

Half an hour later, I was in the long-term parking lot at the Toronto airport. With my backpack on, I awkwardly made my way through the first set of doors, and paused to hold the door for someone approaching from the other side.

"Excuse me ma'am, is that your wallet on the floor?" The woman called out to me. Shocked, I turned around to see the black wallet had fallen out of my coat pocket again. Putting it back, I discovered a zippered vent under the armpit of the jacket where I had been putting my wallet instead of into the pocket. This time, to avoid losing everything if it happened again, I took out my Visa and bankcard and zipped them into the inside pocket of my jacket right beside the Eagle Feather. I was careful to put the wallet full of cash into the actual coat pocket and waited for the bus to the terminal. After arriving I checked my backpack and boarded a plane for Frankfurt, armed with the manuscript of *My Camino* in my carry-on bag, I intended to do one final review on the plane and e-mail any final changes back to Bruce who was waiting to hear from me as soon as I landed.

Buckled-up in my seat, I waited for the plane to take off, watching with the usual disinterest as a flight attendant reviewed the emergency procedures. She explained how to put the oxygen mask on properly. She warned those travelling with children or elderly people to put the mask on them selves first. My immediate reaction was to disagree with this. If my children were with me on the airplane, I would look after saving them before taking oxygen for myself. Then she assured us that we must first give ourselves oxygen, in order to be able to save anyone else. I took this as a clear message for me that going on this journey was about giving to myself, so that I could then give to my children and others when I returned back home.

Once in the air, I pulled out the manuscript and began to read. Incredible memories of my first pilgrimage came flooding back. As a pilgrim, I had recorded the stories in my diary. As a writer, I wrote the stories as the person who experienced them. As an author, I wrote the stories about the experiences of a woman who walked the Camino, and had written about it. Now as a reader, I was reading the stories of a woman who had written a book about her experiences walking the Camino—and she just happened to be me.

After dinner I felt tired and fortunately I slept through most of the six hour flight. As we prepared to land in Frankfurt, it made me think again of Andreas. Because I was so physically close to him, I was nervous and I felt sick to my stomach. I wanted to talk to him right away. Finding a bank of payphones in the middle of the bustling airport, I put some Euros in the slot and dialled his number. To my surprise, he answered the phone.

My heart was beating wildly. I was thrilled to hear his voice. A rush of excitement overcame me. He wanted to see me and right away he asked if we could at least meet during my stop-over in

Frankfurt on the return flight. For some reason, maybe just to be near him again, I agreed to meet. We made plans but the time went by quickly and the payphone used up all the change I had with me. Our conversation ended abruptly and the line cut off before I had a chance to say anything else. Still holding the receiver to my ear, I stood there listening to the dial tone and staring at the phone.

I was confused and no longer sure if Andreas was a part of the journey I had finished, or a part of the journey I was about to embark on. I released my grip and let the phone drop back onto the hook. In my muddled state, I put the black wallet into the outside pocket of my coat. Feeling weak, I fought to hold back my tears. Grabbing my carry-on bag, I paused to gather my composure before returning to the crowded departure gate.

Suddenly, I was bumped hard in the shoulder and spun around. My hands flew out to keep my balance. There were two men. One mumbled something in German. In an instant, they were both gone. I shoved my hand into my pocket. It was empty.

"My wallet," I yelled. "I've been robbed." I called out to the strangers walking by. A dark cloud of despair descended on me. I thought about the Eagle Feather and slipped my hand into the inside pocket of my coat. Thankfully, it was there. My wallet and my money could be replaced; the Eagle Feather could not. I scanned the area for suspicious-looking men. Everyone else was rushing through the cavernous space, caught up in their own personal agendas and the thieves were long gone. And so, with the manuscript in my bag, an Eagle Feather near my heart and no money in my pocket, I began my second pilgrimage on the Camino de Santiago de Compostela.

I remembered reading a story about a Queen in Narvarre who had built a gorgeous arched bridge over the river Arca because so many pilgrims were being robbed and drowned by the crooked fer-

rymen who carried them across the water. Standing there I wondered who, if anyone, was looking after me now.

6

The Perverse Pilgrim

Arriving at my destination in Vigo, Spain after sixteen hours of travel time, I was irritable, tired and my feet were terribly swollen. I disembarked from the small plane onto the runway of the airport. An airline employee guided all the passengers toward a building and through a set of doors, into a bleak and institutional baggage area. Like a jet-set zombie, I stood there waiting for my backpack to appear on the conveyor belt. I watched as each piece of luggage slipped under the black rubber flap and then dropped with a dull thump. One by one, the respective owners hauled their bags away. I watched the same process repeated over and over again, certain each time that the next piece of luggage would be mine.

Time moved very slowly. After about twenty minutes, all of the passengers had left except for an older couple waiting across from me. The three of us stood there with the vain hope that our luggage would magically appear from behind the flap, even though the belt had been empty for several minutes. Then it stopped abruptly with a loud thud and it become dead quiet in the empty room. I looked over at the couple and shrugged. They shook their heads in disappointment. Finally convinced that no other baggage was going to arrive, we walked over to the airline counter. A woman appeared and spoke with the couple in Spanish. I had no idea what they were saying. She went to the back room and returned with forms for them to fill out. I waited patiently.

Standing there, I was reminded of my honeymoon trip to Spain, twenty-five years ago. The day after my husband John and I were married, we left for a two-week vacation in Europe. At the airport in Malaga, we discovered that the airline had lost my luggage. After a long conversation with the staff, who didn't speak English either, John picked up his luggage and I left the airport empty-handed. I didn't really care much about not having my suitcase since we were both happy just being together. Three days later, my luggage arrived at our hotel room along with a bottle of champagne and a box of chocolates, compliments of the airline. That was the beginning of a wonderful twenty-year marriage that eventually ended, like many others, partly because we had both accumulated a lot of emotional baggage over time. Maybe if we had lost our luggage more often, it might have worked out. Now, here I was in Spain, on a new life journey and without any luggage once again. This time I was alone and trying my hardest to be optimistic. Perhaps this was a test to see if I was truly committed to a spiritual quest. I wondered if I would pass. Now it was my turn to fill out the forms which was impossible because they were in Spanish.

"Do you speak English?" I asked the woman. She shook her head. "*Hablo Espanol?*" She asked me in return and I said no. Once she realized we weren't able to communicate, she called another young woman over who spoke perfect English.

"I am very sorry to say that your backpack has not arrived from Madrid," she said, "but we will put a tracer on it. I am sure it will be on the next flight arriving at 23:30 tonight."

"Thank you," I said turning in the direction of the exit sign. I left, clinging to this shred of hope. So far nothing had unfolded the way I had planned. Without any belongings I was feeling more and more like one of the medieval pilgrims, in whose footsteps I was following. My only consolation was that I hadn't put the Eagle Feather in my backpack. And I was comforted by Sherry's words that as long as I had the Eagle Feather, I was in direct connection with the Creator and therefore, safe.

It was cold outside so my immediate concern was to find a place to sleep. I boarded the bus going into Vigo, completely unsure of what I would do when I arrived there. I didn't have accommodation booked, since my plan had been to take a train or bus to Pointe de Lima in Portugal that night and begin the Camino from there the next day. The driver drove crazily, tearing through the narrow, winding streets barely missing lamp posts and parked cars. With great relief I got off at the train station.

Climbing a steep hill, I found a street with a number of small, inexpensive-looking hotels. I went into the first one I came to. The night clerk hovering over his book said there was only one room left with a single bed on the third floor for fifteen Euros. When I didn't respond right away, he shrugged and went back to his book. I don't know exactly why, but I decided not to take the room. After checking many more hotels, I found out the clerk had been right, so I went back and asked for the room. He lifted his head and mumbled that I was too late. The room had been taken.

It was now 9:00 p.m. and I was feeling discouraged. I continued walking until I came to a stoplight. While waiting for it to change to green, I noticed a friendly looking man standing next to me and when I smiled at him, he smiled in return. I asked him if he spoke English and with excitement in his voice and a strong Spanish accent, he said that he did. We introduced ourselves. His English name was William, the same name as my Dad. I asked if he knew where there was an Internet café nearby. He pointed the way and then offered to take me there. We started to walk and when I told him I was doing the Camino, he said he knew all about it and wanted to walk it one day himself. There were a lot of people on the street, all seemingly out for a stroll after dinner. Once we got to the all-night Internet café, I thanked William for his help and we parted ways.

Inside there were banks of computers at empty desks. The heavyset man behind the counter set down his bag of chips and showed me how to log on. I cleared my e-mail messages but decided it was too early in the journey to send any notes to my family and friends. Besides, I couldn't tell them that I had lost my wallet, my money, my backpack and had no place to sleep that night. They'd think I was crazy and I wouldn't blame them, I was beginning to think so myself. There was still work to be done on my manuscript so I took out the hard copy. It took several more hours, going slowly through each page, reading it aloud. At 11:00 p.m. I stopped working to catch the late bus back to the airport in anticipation of being reunited with my simple pilgrim belongings.

The city was dark and the street was quiet. I crossed the road and waited alone at the bus stop. As a pilgrim on the road to Santiago, my backpack actually provided some level of security. The government of Spain has specific laws against exploiting or harming a pilgrim in any way. Standing there, in the city without it, I could easily be taken for a tourist and become a target for a mugging again. So far, I had already been stripped of most of my material possessions. I felt exposed, alone and vulnerable.

Once again the universe provided a maniacal bus driver who got us to the airport in less than fifteen minutes. The woman who'd served me earlier was nowhere to be found. I was told to go see the Security Guard since the counter was officially closed. Unable to speak effectively with the Guard on duty, I showed him the receipt I had been given earlier for my lost luggage. Once he saw this, he called someone else over to translate. This was followed by another conversation in Spanish after which he made a phone call. When he was finished talking on the phone, he escorted me to the luggage room and unlocked the door. There were two bags that hadn't been claimed from the last flight; neither of them was mine. I tried to maintain my composure but my eyes quickly filled with tears as I walked back to the lounge empty-handed.

I decided to wait at the airport that night so I could be there for the first flight in from Madrid at 6:30 a.m. in the morning. Near a section of vacant chairs in the waiting area, I took off my boots for the first time since I left Toronto. My feet were damp and already aching. I curled up on the bank of chairs, resting my head on my carry-on bag. Pulling my coat over me and tucking in my feet to keep warm, I fell quickly into a restless sleep.

It seemed like only a few minutes had passed when I was awakened by a deep voice. It was the same Security Guard speaking sternly to me in Spanish. He pointed to the main door telling me the airport was closed and that I must leave the building. I begged him to let me stay but without showing any emotion, he stood there firmly pointing to the doors. He watched while I put on my boots and gathered my things together. I got up and followed him to the main doors. He unlocked them and I stepped out into the damp, cold night.

By now it was after 1:00 a.m. and the buses had stopped running. A solitary taxi was parked across the road, the driver's head tilted back against the seat as he slept. Gently, I knocked lightly on the window but it startled him awake. When he rolled down the window, I asked him to take me back to Vigo. The sleepy taxi driver dropped me off on the main street near the all-night Internet café. I paid him with the only cash I had and walked up the now-familiar hill. For the second time that day, I arrived in the city without my backpack, money and even worse, it was the middle of the night with no place to sleep. I felt like a homeless person. There was a bank machine and I withdrew fifty Euros. It felt good to have some cash in my pocket again.

Further along the street there was a *taberna*. I went into the restaurant and sat down. It was filled with young people laughing and having a good time but they were smoking cigarettes. The clouds of smoke made breathing difficult for me because of my asthma. I worried about having an attack since I hadn't brought a puffer. My nose started to get stuffed up and I soon developed a horrible headache. Everyone around me was drinking beer or wine. Sherry had said the Eagle Feather should not be exposed to alcohol or mood-altering drugs. In Spain, most of the restaurants and cafes serve alcohol anytime throughout the day and night. Since I wasn't sure what I should do to protect it, I created my own guidelines. I decided that as long as the Eagle Feather was in its red fabric home, it would be protected from any exposure to alcohol or mood altering drugs. I trusted that the Creator was guiding me in this decision.

I ordered a *cafe con leche*, drank it quickly and left. Back I went to the all-night Internet café where there was no smoking. The owner nodded when I walked in and I sat down at a computer near the back of the room. Taking out the manuscript, I proceeded to finish the edits and composed a note to Bruce to send along with them. Although I said I wanted to be alone on this journey, I was already beginning to miss his company.

It was now 4:20 a.m. and I was sleepy and hungry. With no other options, I returned to the restaurant filled with young couples and cigarette smoke and sat near the door hoping to get some of the fresh air that drifted in. I ordered a hamburger. A large plate of complimentary olives arrived first and I devoured them immediately. They served me a home-made hamburger on white bread with French fries. The food was delicious and true to my big-family upbringing, I ate everything on my plate.

Hardly able to keep my eyes awake I tried to read a Spanish newspaper, surprising myself at how much I thought I understood. Somehow I managed to pass the hours waiting for this never-ending night to be over. Finally, hours later I caught the early morning bus back to the airport with a renewed sense of hope that my backpack would be there.

7

The Journey Begins

It was still dark when I returned to the airport for the third time. The young woman who'd helped me out the first time was on duty. She motioned for me to wait while she went to the back room to check on the luggage that had arrived on the morning flight. She returned with bad news. I shook my head in disbelief. Seeing my reaction, she suggested that my backpack might be locked in the security room. A Security Guard would have to let me in, but their shift didn't begin for another hour. I pleaded with her, explaining how I must be on the train to Pointe de Lima which was leaving in an hour. Raising her finger, she signalled for me to wait. She walked over to the café where the Security Guards were eating their break-fast. Within minutes she returned.

"They will be back in about a half hour," she said.

"That's too late. I'll miss my train." I pleaded as my eyes filled with tears. Ever since being mugged in Frankfurt and losing my backpack, I hadn't acknowledged my emotions in any way. Now I couldn't stop the rivulets of tears that ran down my cheeks. I felt like a fool standing there in the middle of the airport crying over a missing backpack. From behind me, I heard a loud, demanding voice speaking in Spanish. Wiping the tears from my eyes, I turned to see the Security Guard leaning against the wall. He was jangling the keys in his pocket, I suspected he was trying to show me that he was in charge. He unlocked the security door and I followed him in.

He stopped and pointed to the suitcases on the floor. My backpack wasn't there. I shook my head. He shrugged his shoulders as if to say there was nothing else he could do. I left the luggage area, again empty-handed.

Never, even on my first Camino, had I felt so completely alone and I hadn't even begun walking yet. I kept asking myself different questions such as: Why is this happening to me now? What's the lesson for me? Is this a sign from the Camino? Am I expecting too much? Am I being humbled into surrendering before I go on the path? Why am I attracting this to me? I had no answers but at that moment, I seriously considered just turning around and going back home. Instead I went outside where the bus was waiting to return to Vigo. I boarded it and sat at the back. Looking out the window as buildings and homes passed by, I thought about what my kids would think of me if they knew I was spending the night wandering around from a restaurant, to an Internet café, on a bus, in a taxi, and worst of all, getting kicked out for sleeping in an airport. The only consolation I had was that I was in the presence of the Eagle Feather. According to Sherry, I was protected.

Prior to leaving Canada, a woman named Judith had sent an e-mail to a Camino list service of which I was a member, asking if anyone would be in Santiago on Easter Sunday. She had walked the Camino in the past, was visiting that weekend as a tourist and wanted to share Easter dinner with a pilgrim. I responded to her e-mail and we arranged to meet at 2:00 p.m. on Sunday afternoon in the lobby of the famous Parador Hotel. To make it there in time to meet Judith, I'd have to leave by tomorrow.

With forced optimism, I considered the possibility of beginning to walk without my backpack. I placed the contents of my overnight bag on the seat next to me. Taking stock, I made a mental note of the things I needed and the things I could do without. The two-hundred page manuscript, I would mail home. I needed my diary, camera, water bottle, pen, toothbrush, toothpaste and a hairbrush. I could buy more toiletries, another sleeping bag, a backpack and some extra clothes in one of the larger cities along the way. I'd also need an extra pair of socks, underwear and some Vaseline for my feet. With some first aid products for my blisters, I concluded that I could easily be on my way. Simply by making the decision to begin walking, I felt more in control and this made the whole situation seem less stressful. I was once again excited about embarking on the Camino.

The bus stopped at the train station. I ran in as fast as I could to catch the last train to Pointe de Lima, Portugal. The departure board showed my train was on Track 5. I didn't have the time to buy a ticket, so I ran directly toward the track. Before I got there, the doors closed and the train pulled away. It was the only train leaving for that destination that day. Still determined not to give up, I decided to make my way to the Portuguese city of Valenca, which was close to the Spanish border. It was roughly one-hundred and thirty kilometres to Santiago; I could easily walk that distance in six days and give me enough time to meet Judith on Easter Sunday. From there I would travel another ninety kilometres to Fisterra, the furthest westerly point of Spain. Before Christopher Columbus discovered the world was round, the pilgrims of the past believed this place was the end of the world. After they arrived in Fisterra, they would collect a scallop shell from the sea and wear it proudly as proof that they were Camino pilgrims. Since then the scallop shell has become the international symbol of a pilgrim. Modern-day pilgrims don't usually walk the return route, so most purchase a scallop shell before embarking on their journey and wear it proudly along the way.

Subsequently, I planned to follow the sea-side pilgrim route to the coastal village of Muxia on the ominously named, Costa da Morte or the Coast of Death. Once there I would turn around and begin walking the return journey in the reverse direction, like the pilgrims of the past. I planned to end up where I had started in Valenca, Portugal, covering almost five hundred kilometres in total. Now all I had to do was to figure out how to get to Portugal that morning.

When I asked the station attendant where the bus terminal was located, he asked where I was going. When I told him he strongly suggested I consider taking a taxi instead of waiting hours for the next bus. I took his advice. I went outside to the taxi stand and approached the first car. Leaning into the open window, I asked the driver what he would charge to drive me there.

"Twenty-five Euros," he said with a thick accent and a welcoming smile. I opened the door and got in.

"Let's go," I said excitedly. As soon as we pulled away, I got comfortable in the back seat and checked to make sure the Eagle Feather was safely stored in my pocket. I loosened the laces of my boots to air my feel. Hot spots had developed on the balls of my feet and this was the first indication that blisters were forming. From past experience, I knew how important it was to care for my feet, but with all the distractions I had encountered so far, I'd completely neglected them. With my head resting against the back of the seat, relieved I was finally on my journey, I dozed off.

"*Hola*," the driver called out and I startled awake from my short sleep. "Valenca," he said as he stopped the car. Looking out the window I could see it had been raining heavily. Morning mist hovered over the old city. Not wanting to leave the security of the taxi until I was sure of where I was going, I hesitated to get out.

"*A qui el Camino?*" I attempted to ask him where the path began. He pointed down the cobblestone road to a stone wall that looked like the outside of a fort. I paid the fare and once I was out of the car, he drove away quickly. It appeared as though I was on the main street in the city of Valenca. I stood alone in front of a quaint Portuguese linen shop admiring the hand-embroidered linens in the window. It was just after 9:00 a.m. and the retail stores were still closed.

My feet were burning and I desperately needed to find a store to buy socks. Still dressed in the clothes I wore on the flight two days ago, I felt grungy and in need of a bath and clean clothes. Nonetheless, I had decided to embark on my journey, so I scanned the area for directional yellow arrows or a scallop shell symbol on a blue tile that were sometimes mounted on buildings or imbedded into the sidewalks. Within moments, I found a yellow directional arrow that confirmed I was finally on my way.

A stone gateway led me into an old fortress. I followed the path through a tunnel and eventually back outside to a spectacular view of a bridge across the river Mino to Tui, Spain. I crossed the long bridge that now carries both vehicles and pilgrims into Spain.

Entering the old city, I was in awe of the magnificent Romanesque and Gothic styled Cathedral of Santa Maria de Tui. The stunning façade is dedicated to the glory of the Virgin Mary. Stepping through the enormous wooden doors, built in the twelfth century, I entered the vestibule of the historic church. The familiar aroma of incense reminded me of my Catholic upbringing. Instinctively clasped my hands together and began to pray. The pilgrim-worn stones below my feet gave me the feeling I was stepping into the intentions of the millions of pilgrims who had walked this way before me.

The 900 year old Cathedral was modeled after the even older Cathedral in Santiago. There was a chapel and oddly it was dedicated to Saint James, the warrior. Sadly, he had a dark side to his story of converting the north of Spain to Christianity. He was also known as Matamoros, the Moor slayer. At the front altar, I lit a candle and prayed to God, asking for divine guidance on my journey. Then I spent a moment staring in awe at the elaborate ornamentation.

On the way out, a tall, neatly-dressed man stood behind a small table covered with Camino-related books and postcards for sale. I took out the *credential* or pilgrim passport I had ordered through the Canadian Company of Pilgrims office in Toronto. It was a simple plastic coated booklet with pages provided for the stamps that would be given at each village along the way. This would prove I had walked the minimum one hundred kilometres on the Camino, the distance required to qualify as a genuine pilgrim. Once my stamped credential was presented to the Pilgrim Office in Santiago, they would issue a certificate of completion called a Compostela. Standing there, I opened the booklet to the first page and the man stamped it.

"*Gracias*," I said, feeling proud that my journey as a pilgrim had finally begun. Back outside it was sunny and around fourteen degrees Celsius—the perfect temperature for walking. According to the booklet, I only had nineteen kilometres to walk on my first day. Before I knew it I was leaving the city of Tui and was soon surrounded by trees experiencing the silence and peacefulness of the forest. The only sound was the gentle crinkle of dried leaves as the wind brushed them along. The fragrant scent of the damp air was familiar and comforting. It was like I was coming home to Mother Earth. I picked up a stone and as I had done so many times before, I imagined putting my sorrow into it and then set it down on the path, letting my sorrow go. I picked up a stone for each of my three daughters and following the same ritual, I set their sorrow on the Camino path too. It was my gift to them from afar.

After about an hour, the residual fatigue of jetlag began to weigh on me. I wanted to go to sleep. A narrow and worn path veered off to the right and I followed it toward the sound of loud rushing water. It led to the bank of a stream where I set down my carry-on bag, curled up in the wild flowers and immediately fell asleep. It was surreal and dreamlike, as though I was on the yellow brick road with Dorothy in *The Wizard of Oz.*

Hours later, I was startled by a loud cracking sound somewhere in the forest. I jumped up, wondering if this was just a dream. The pressure on my bladder told me I wasn't dreaming. I had to pee. I stood up and unzipped my hiking pants while shuffling over to a bush. Without Kleenex or toilet paper to wipe myself, I grabbed a leaf off a bush, hoping it wasn't some foreign version of poison ivy. Crouching down by the water to wash my hands in the icy water, I wondered what the rest of the world doing at this moment.

8

Sorrow Stones

From behind me, the sound of young voices approached, the music of their language was enchanting. A group of five teenagers were walking together. There were four boys with a girl leading the way. Seeing them reminded me of how much I missed being around my daughters friends after they moved away from my home. The girl caught up to me and I asked if she spoke English. She said they were from Madrid and had all learned some English in school. They were anxious to practice with me and each of them took turns asking me questions and answering mine. I found out they were friends who'd decided to walk this section of the Camino as a group in celebration of Easter week.

One of the boys, wearing a red bandana tied around his head, caught my attention. He was more reserved, than the others but listened with keen interest. They soon tired of my limited language skills and I waved them on.

Before long, however, I caught up with the young man with the red bandana. It seemed as though he had purposefully slowed, waiting for me to catch up. He was quite tall with a youthful build and jet-black hair. He was wearing running shoes and carried a small backpack.

"I'm Sue, from Canada," I said politely introducing myself. He looked at me, not comprehending my simple name, and tried to repeat it several different ways. In European countries, I'd discovered, they were not accustomed to saying one syllable names. "It's Su-san," I repeated clearly enunciating the syllables.

"Susannah?" he asked. I nodded thinking maybe on this Camino it would be easier if I just called myself Susannah. After all, it's the Latin version of Susan and the name that was written on my Compostela when I completed the French Route.

"My name is Marius," he said with a slight accent. Then he said this was his second time walking the Camino. That surprised me since he seemed so very young. He was twenty-three and two years ago had walked from Sarria to Santiago, covering more than one hundred kilometres.

"Why is someone your age walking the Camino again?" I asked with curiosity. With his head bowed, he spoke in a soft voice. He told me that his mother died a few weeks ago. My heart suddenly became heavy with sadness for this young man. He said that she was on one of the trains attacked during the Madrid bombings on March 11th. My heart started beating faster filling my entire body with anger and sorrow at the same time.

"She didn't die right away," Marius continued, "she lived for six days in a coma and then passed away peacefully in her sleep. She was forty-five years old." She was almost the same age as me, I realized. I thought about how my daughters would handle being without their mother. This triggered my emotional maternal instincts and I wanted to take him home with me. He said he had been very close to his mother. Before the bombing, he'd mentioned to her that he was considering another pilgrimage on the Camino. She had strongly encouraged him to go and that was why he was walking it again with his friends. I wanted to help him in some way but I wasn't sure what I could do. Then I remembered the story of the Sorrow Stones.

"Marius, I have a story I'd like to share with you." He nodded in agreement and listened closely as I began talking. "During my first pilgrimage on the French Route of the Camino, I noticed there were piles of stones all along the path where I walked. One day at dinner, I asked a group of pilgrims if anyone knew why the stones were there. A German pilgrim named Andreas said that he knew a story about the stones and he shared it with me," I paused. "He said, 'It is said that if you pick up a stone and put your sorrow into it, when you place it down you leave some of your sorrow behind.' I was moved my this idea and decided to try it."

Marius looked directly at me and asked, "Did it work?"

"That's exactly what I wanted to find out," I answered and then continued. "The next day when I started walking, the first thing I did was to look for a stone. When I found one, I picked it up but I wasn't sure how to put my sorrow into it. I rubbed the smooth stone between my fingers and just imagined I could. When it felt right, I set the stone down on the path. Right away there was a shift in energy, as if my sorrow was leaving me. It felt so good I wanted to pick up another stone right away. So I did. I picked up one for my oldest daughter, Tara. I rubbed the stone and imagined moving her sorrow into it. Then I set it down on the path and picked up another stone for my middle daughter, Meghan. After I walked with it for a while, I did the same thing. Finally I picked up another stone for my youngest daughter, Simone, and left her sorrow there, too. Even though I didn't know what their sorrow was or how much they had, I felt it was the perfect gift I could give them from the Camino."

As we walked, I bent over and picked up a stone from the path. We continued to walk through the forest. I told Marius that I picked up stones everyday and by the end of my journey, I felt like I had no sorrow left at all. It was like I was in a state of grace. I explained how I met Andreas near the end of my journey and I told him what a profound effect his story had on me. Then he informed me that he didn't actually believe in the Sorrow Stones.

"Why not?" Marius looked puzzled.

"He said someone had told the story to him and he was simply sharing it with me." I told Marius that through this I had learned it wasn't about whether Andreas believed in the Sorrow Stones or not. It was only about what I believed that really mattered. "In the end it's just a story," I said. Marius seemed comforted by my words. I gave him the stone I had picked up earlier. We walked in silence for a while and I watched as he rubbed the stone between his fingers.

"Marius!" His school friend called out to him. He turned to me and said, "Thanks Susannah. I have to go now." Waving goodbye to me he ran ahead to catch up with the others. Then he stopped and placed the stone on the path. I stood there watching him and a flood of maternal emotions washed over me, filling my eyes with tears. Searching the ground, I found another smooth, gray stone and picked it up. I started walking again feeling the cold smoothness of it in my fingers. When it felt right, I set it down on the path letting my own sorrow go.

9

A Religious Vocation

Hours passed. It became very warm walking in the afternoon sun and I was perspiring. My glasses kept slipping down my nose. I crossed a stone bridge and stopped to take a short break. Sitting alone, I took off my jacket, boots and socks. I ate a crunchy red apple and washed it down with lukewarm water. Then I rolled my pants up to mid-calf like pedal-pushers and resumed walking.

An hour later, reaching an intersection in a small village there was a sign for a restaurant that was about fifty metres off the path. I decided to go. It was noon but the restaurant was empty. I ordered a *cafe con leche* and then used the bathroom. I sat at the bar to watch the news on a television mounted high on the wall. Unable to see clearly, I went to put on my glasses but couldn't find them in my pockets or my bag. They were gone. I remembered taking them off while sitting on the stone bridge—at least two kilometres back in the opposite direction. Since I had trouble seeing distances, I knew that I couldn't live without my glasses. Gathering my things, I left the restaurant and walked back, scanning the dirt path as I retraced my steps. I looked everywhere for them but because my vision was blurred everything I saw on the ground somehow looked like my glasses. I picked up sticks, leaves, an old banana peel, even stones by mistake.

While I walked I could feel hot spots on the soles of my feet. When I stopped for a break to air my sweaty feet, I was shocked to see the skin had become pink. I knew I was in deep trouble. To prevent further blistering, I had to keep my feet dry. I began walking barefoot hoping the fresh air would help. The soles of my feet were sensitive at first so it took some adjusting to get used to the rough ground. Unfortunately, I never did find my glasses and I eventually gave up. All that backtracking had added about four extra kilometres to that day. When I decided to walk the Camino in both directions, I didn't know I'd be retracing my steps so early in my journey.

Walking alone gave me plenty of time to think about my life. I recalled the time when I was eight years old and had first become aware of the idea of a life purpose. It all started one summer day at church.

As a child I was raised Roman Catholic and every Sunday morning my Mum made all of her children get up early to prepare to go to Mass. There were five girls and one boy, my brother Larry. Church was a big deal in our house. We had special clothes to wear and good shoes that were never worn at any other time. On Saturday night, my sisters and I washed and curled our hair for Mass the next day while Dad would often fall asleep on the couch after getting home late from the bar. He never joined us at church.

That one Sunday morning, as each child was dressed, Mum sent us outside to wait on the front porch until everyone was ready. She yelled from the other end of the house, "If you get your good clothes dirty, there'll be Hell to pay." I didn't know what she meant by that, but I knew the Devil lived in Hell. Since I was the black sheep of the family, the one that was always talking too much and getting into trouble for doing things no one else did, I was sure that the Devil lurked around me all the time.

As the second-oldest child, I felt responsible for my younger siblings. Once they were out on the porch, my sister Patricia and I would get them to line up in a row. I knew they weren't old enough to fight the Devil's temptations and I believed if I didn't watch over the little ones then the Devil would tempt them to get dirty and snatch them all off to Hell.

Mum eventually showed up on the porch, still getting dressed on the run. She moved a bit more slowly that day because she was eight months pregnant with my sister, Kelly. We obediently followed her, marching up Lansdowne Avenue, along Dundas Street and climbed the wide stone stairs entering the door at the side. Mum pushed the thick wooden door open and we all piled into the vestibule at St. Helen's Roman Catholic Church. Once inside my three-year old sister Joanne, pointed her finger at the stone font and pleaded with me to lift her up. Eventually I did so she could dip her finger in to bless herself, but what she really wanted to do was drink it. The next thing I knew, my sister Donna wanted some, then Larry and all the other kids were lined up for their turn. Quickly running out of patience, my Mum sternly pointed her finger to the front of the church and we all knew it was time to go.

Obediently, we trailed behind as Mum led us up the center aisle. Taking Joanne's tiny hand, I walked with her, shuffling my feet so that I didn't step on Patty and Donna's heels ahead of me. Among the congregation, heads turned and people pointed. There was whispering all around us as we passed. I knew Mum was so proud of us but I was embarrassed at the way people stared. It was like we were part of a parade or a freak show. I knew they were judging us and I worried about what they were saying. I was horrified to think that maybe they knew the gas was turned off and we had no hot water because my Dad couldn't pay the bill. Did they know my Dad drank too much and he was asleep on the couch at home? Were they questioning why my Mum had so many children and was pregnant with yet another one? It was many years later when I asked my Mum why she decided to have so many children when it was such a struggle and there wasn't enough money to go around?

"It's God's work," she'd said. "I don't question it." Then she told me that the Church wouldn't allow her to take birth control pills. After bearing seven children in ten years, her doctor insisted for her health that she stop having children. She had no other choice but, but to take the birth control pill. This was considered a sin by the Catholic Church. She went to Confession and begged the parish priest to give her absolution, but he wouldn't. When she told her doctor, he gave her the name of a more liberal priest who she went to see. There she was finally given the absolution she desired. My Mum continued to go to Church regularly and although she had reconciled this sin through the church, she lived those years of her life wracked with guilt and shame for not wanting to have more than seven children.

After she told me that story, I vowed that I'd be dutiful about going to Confession but once I was old enough and couldn't be forced to, then I'd never go again. I trusted that I could personally ask God for absolution from my sins without the politics of the Church getting involved.

As usual, that day Mum marched us right up to the very first row on the left and she waited until we had all slid along the pew. One by one we sat down. Then she pulled the wooden kneeler forward and motioned for us to follow her as she kneeled down, blessed herself and began to say the Rosary. I watched as her lips moved quickly saying the words she had spoken for a lifetime. She looked over at us with her lips squeezed together and her eyebrows knitted; an unmistakable look that warned us to start praying and not to misbehave. We were obedient children and did exactly as we were told.

During the sermon that day, I was admiring the stained glass windows and daydreaming when I heard a word that caught my attention. The priest was talking about vocation. He suggested that we should consider what our vocation in life is and then live it, just like the saints did. This was something I had never considered doing. As far as everyone else was concerned, it was assumed that I'd eventually get married and have a big family, just like Mum. This assumption became a serious dilemma for me because I'd already decided that I wasn't going to only be a wife and a mother. That day, I listened with keen interest and hope about having a vocation, only to realize that the priest was specifically talking to the boys and the men in the congregation. The church was looking for prospects interested in entering the seminary to become priests.

Nothing was said to the young women who were at Mass that day about their vocation. I wondered why women became nuns and if that was a vocation, too. Even at the age of eight, it seemed like the nuns in the church took a back seat as leaders, compared to the role of a priest in the congregation. Nuns were assigned the important roles of serving, caring for the sick and teaching, but it seemed that only priests stood in front of the congregation as leaders. I wondered if this meant that their role was deemed more important than that of being a nun.

The idea of having a vocation in my life was very appealing, but I didn't want to be a housewife or a nun and they seemed to be my only options. I felt I had something else to offer the world, although I didn't know what it was. What I took away from the priest's sermon that day was that a vocation is a calling to give your life to Christ, but only if you are a man. What was I, as a woman, supposed to do if I had a vocation but wasn't prepared to give my life to the church? That day, I began a life-long quest to understand my vocation. As I grew up and became a young woman, I struggled to figure out how to I could be a leader, like the priest I saw at church.

10

Blisters and Bunk Beds

According to the pilgrim guidebook, the city of O Porrino was the destination for my first day of walking. The large industrial buildings lining both sides of the road, often set back on the property, made me feel disconnected from both nature and the Camino path itself. Sufficiently bored with the landscape, I repeated the same thoughts over and over again. It wasn't easy to calm my mind so I distracted myself by counting each step. When I arrived at the bridge on the edge of the city, I had numbered twelve-hundred steps and had walked just over a kilometre, giving me some perspective on what I had just done. Drivers passing by called out encouragement for me to keep going.

"Arriva! Arriva!" They yelled while honking their horns and I'd wave back to them. I'd traveled almost twenty kilometres already that day and welcomed their support. The people who live along the Camino path seem to have a vocation of their own, helping pilgrims as they pass through their village. They're rewarded when the pilgrims arrive in Santiago to hug the statue of the Apostle, giving thanks to all the people who helped them.

Since my feet had become blistered from the early days of walking in the wrong socks, I stopped at the first store I came to and bought the ingredients needed to soak my feet. On my travels, I'd learned of an ancient healing solution for blisters that has been used by pilgrims for centuries. It consisted of sea salt, vinegar and warm water. I hadn't showered in three days so I hoped the pilgrim refugio (or albergue, as they were called in this region of Spain) would provide me with a towel since the high absorbency one I'd packed was in my missing backpack.

Hours later, I finally arrived in the beautiful old city of O Porrino. I followed the yellow arrows through the outskirts of the city, as the sun was slowly setting. Normally, as part of my own pilgrim ritual, this was the time of day when I'd stop and meditate on being grateful. But today, the pain from the blisters that had developed on my feet was unbearable and gratitude was the last thing on my mind.

The albergue was at the far end of the city, near train tracks. The door was locked so I knocked on the closest window. An older male pilgrim appeared and gladly opened the door for me. I thanked him and went to the registration counter where I signed my name in the guest book and stamped my own credential. I took off my boots, left them at the door and went upstairs to the dorm rooms. There were separate rooms for women and men with rows of gray metal bunk beds. No other female pilgrims were there.

Having no sleeping bag, I found some extra blankets and made myself a bed. Thankfully, the mattresses looked brand new. One blanket was used to cover the mattress as a sheet and another was placed on top for warmth. By folding a thin blanket, I made a pillow. Slipping the Eagle Feather inside my carry-on bag, I took it downstairs with me. I found the showers and used some of the dish soap from the kitchen to wash myself. There were no towels, so I dried myself with a cotton table cloth that I found in a cupboard. After brushing my teeth, I went back to the kitchen and found a large metal bowl under the sink. I filled it with warm water, added some sea salt and vinegar I found in the cupboard and eased my aching body onto a kitchen chair. I slipped my tired, burning feet into the solution. At first the pain from the blisters stung and then my feet began to throb. I tried not to think about how I could possibly walk another four-hundred and fifty kilometres over the next eighteen days with my feet in this condition.

Four young Spanish men entered the kitchen through the back door talking loudly. One of them, Caesar, spoke a bit of English so he introduced himself and his friends Richard, John and his brother Manuel. They had just returned from the hospital because Manuel had injured his ankle while walking and had to go home. I chatted with them as Manuel limped upstairs to pack. I told them about losing my backpack. Gallantly, Caesar took out his cell phone and said he'd call the airport. I was grateful for his offer. He spoke to someone there and found out my backpack still hadn't arrived. Richard offered to lend me his bulky sweatshirt to sleep in and I gratefully accepted. It was the beginning of April and the nights were still very cold. They were going out for dinner and invited me to join them. It was very kind of them to include me but declined their offer, preferring to rest.

After they had left, I washed my socks and underwear, hung them and my other clothes up on the railing of the bunk bed to air out and got ready for bed. I slipped into Richard's warm sweatshirt and tucked the Eagle Feather along with my wallet under the blanket beside me. Holding it close to me, I thought about what Sherry said about praying to the Creator at sunrise and I decided I should begin that ritual tomorrow. By 9:00 p.m. I was fast asleep.

Eleven hours later, I woke up feeling pleasantly well-rested but I had missed the sunrise. The first thing I did was check for the Eagle Feather. Then I examined my feet to find that two huge water blisters had developed on my heels and the skin was pink. I would have to do some pilgrim blister surgery. Quietly, I slipped out of bed and got dressed. Downstairs I found a first aid kit, threaded a sewing needle, soaked it with iodine and then carefully poked a hole in the blister puncturing it so the fluid could escape. I left the iodine-soaked thread inside the blister to wick away any fluids and then wrapped it with gauze and tape. When I went back to the room to gather my things, I placed Richard's sweatshirt folded neatly on the bed with a thank-you note, then hobbled downstairs to the kitchen to fill my water bottle.

Outside, the sun was shining brightly and people were rushing around. In a small grocery shop, I bought some bread, cheese and a flaky pastry with cooked meat inside. The overnight bag I had was small so I had to be conscious of how much food I could carry. I found a store that had cheap cotton sports socks so I bought them and immediately put a pair on. Now I had everything I needed. Arriving at the Post Office, I finally mailed home the manuscript which substantially lightened my load.

Back on the path on my way to Redondela, I experienced a brief moment of panic at the thought I'd never see my backpack again. It was my second day of walking and still early in the morning, so I stopped on the path. Setting my bag down, I took the Eagle Feather out of its red cloth home for the first time since I arrived in Spain. My thoughts drifted to how I should honour the Eagle Feather that I was carrying. Sherry had said her *Nokomis* (Grandmother) would always pray to the Creator facing east, preferably as the sun was rising. Sherry told me to begin with the words *Miigwech Creator*—which means thank you Creator. It felt strange to hold it and I wasn't sure how to pray to the Creator or what I should say. Awkwardly, I repeated the words.

"*Miigwech Creator,*" I said and then because I was afraid of losing it, I quickly put it back in its red cloth home. I placed it in the leather pouch and stored it in the inside pocket of my coat. Pulling my backpack up over my shoulders I set out to walk.

My thoughts turned to what criteria I should use to select the recipient of the sacred Eagle Feather. How would I best decide who would be the one to receive it? Sherry said that in her dream, when I met them it was dusty. She also said the person would come from another country. I thought the person should also be a pilgrim. They should also be very clear about their purpose in life. It was most imperative that they be respectful of the First Nation people and have a desire to share their teachings with the world. As I thought more about it, my list grew longer. How, I wondered, was I going to find someone to fit all of these qualifications? Then I remembered Sherry had said the recipient would acknowledge me with the virtues of kindness, honour and love. I knew I would need to pay close attention.

In the distance, church bells were playing the hymn Ave Maria, the same music that was played at my wedding twenty-three years ago and at my sister Donna's funeral. No one was on the path with me so I sang the lyrics as loudly as I could so that she could hear me and know that she wasn't alone. My eyes filled with tears and then I started to cry from deep within. Donna's children, Joshua, Kyle and Brett, had lost their mother to cancer when she was only forty years old. The boys were only five, seven and nine when she died. It had been a very difficult time for everyone, especially my Mum. Donna often showed up in my thoughts when I walked my first Camino. Her loving spirit seemed to channel through me, guiding me through some of the most difficult times. She was fifteen months younger than me. I remembered when Donna was a child she was always afraid of things like the dark, walking home from school by herself, sleeping alone, and even as a young girl, she was afraid of dying. Me, I was the tough kid who never got sick and wasn't afraid of anything or at least I didn't let on to anyone when I was.

Climbing upward by way of the village of Enxertade, my emotions waned. I arrived at a lovely chapel called Santiaguino de Antas. Unfortunately, it was closed so I moved on. My breathing became laboured as I climbed even higher and gasping for air, I started to focus on each breath, using meditation practice to calm myself. In the silence between each thought, I was aware of the noise of the rustle of the leaves in the trees. Feeling connected to the well-worn ground below my feet and the immense sky above comforted me. I followed the trail to the edge of a lush forest with a picnic area complete with tables made of thick slabs of beautiful pink granite. This region of Spain was known for its production of Rosa Granite—pink stone.

The view of the ancient city of Redondela, nestled in the valley below was absolutely breathtaking. I stood still, opening my heart to allow myself to take in the beauty of it all at a cellular level and trust everything would be fine. From the top of the mountain, I felt a cool breeze on my face. I could see the distance I had yet to travel to the albergue. I knew from my travels walking in the Pyrenees Mountains in France that it would be more difficult walking down the mountain, then it was climbing up. I found a long stick in the forest to use for support and started the long descent. By taking small steps, I reduced the risk of my weight pressing forward and putting additional strain on my knees. A knee injury was the last thing I needed.

Reaching the outskirts of the city, I looked everywhere for the yellow arrows or signs directing me to the albergue where I would sleep that night. The pilgrims on the Camino were a source of income for the Spaniards and because of this, the arrows often led us through the entire city first. Not unlike the way milk and eggs are positioned at the back of a grocery store so you have to go through the entire store to get what you really want.

While walking on the sidewalk through Redondela, I caught up to four other pilgrims. One of them introduced himself as Marcello, a Brazilian. He lived in England and was visiting his Godfather in Vigo. He introduced me to the others but unfortunately they couldn't speak any English. We soon arrived at the albergue, a gorgeous sixteenth century renovated building named the Casa da

Torre. The sign on the door of the albergue said it opened at 5:00 p.m. and now it was now only 3:30 p.m. so we found a bench and sat in the warm sun waiting patiently. In the meantime, I told Marcello about my still missing backpack. He offered to call the airline for me—the second pilgrim to be so generous. He came back from the pay phone smiling because they had found my backpack.

I jumped up. I was thrilled at the idea of having my simple pilgrim belongings with me again. Immediately, I hailed a taxi and we drove to the airport. At the airline counter I handed my receipt to the same woman I had dealt with before. She returned in a few minutes with my errant backpack. I opened it and quickly rifled through it, overjoyed that everything was there and in perfect shape. I slipped it over my shoulders and noticed that after carrying the small overnight bag, the weight of my full backpack—about ten kilos—was a shock. I heaved it into the waiting taxi and we drove back to the albergue. Lugging my pack up the stairs to the third floor bunk room, I passed an art gallery poster with the word Plume and a photo of a feather gently falling to the ground. I wondered aloud at the possible significance of this coincidence.

Following a typically cool albergue shower, I went outside to the pay phone and called my Mum.

"Hello. Who is it?" she said in a weak voice.

"It's me, Susan," I said, gently yelling into the phone. I had noticed that as she was getting older, I had to speak to her in simple language as she was more easily confused. "I'm calling from Spain, Mum. Everything is fine except that I was mugged at the airport in Frankfurt and they stole my wallet." As soon as I said those words, I wished I hadn't.

"Are you alright? Do you need some money?" She asked in a worried state. It was only thirty seconds into the call and I could tell she was crying.

"Mum, everything's alright," I assured her, "there are many people who are caring for me. Don't worry. I have been leaving stones for you on the path," I said.

"Be careful, Susan." Her voice trailed off.

"I will Mum." I said and then I heard dial tone. It wasn't usual for us to say we loved each other on the phone but that day I wanted to say it. It was too late. She had hung up the phone. Her emotional reaction to my situation made me wonder why I was there, putting up with the hardships. Maybe it was me who was confused and not her.

Then, I called my oldest daughter, Tara, who was now twenty-one years old and finishing her last year as a philosophy major at a university in London, Ontario. We had a great relationship and even though she hadn't completely understood why I was going back on the Camino she respected my decision. I was terribly disappointed when I reached her voice mail and I left a rambling, emotional message.

"Tara, it's Mum. I'm here in Spain on the Camino … well, you know that already. How are you doing? I just arrived at the albergue for the pilgrims in a small town. I walked about twenty kilometres today. Had a few problems getting here; I was mugged at the airport and then the airline lost my luggage. Don't worry, I'm okay but I lost all my money. Weather is perfect. It's sunny and around fourteen degrees Celsius. Not much rain expected, so that's good for walking. I think you would love the Spanish countryside, Tara. It's a lot like Ireland. Well, I really wanted to talk to you live because I miss you. I love you. Say hi to Darrell. Love you." I hung up the phone and took a long deep breath.

Then I dialled the lengthy code for the international calling card again and called the home of my ex-husband John, where my other two daughters Meghan and Simone now lived. I waited eagerly for one of them to answer the phone. Meghan, my middle daughter was nineteen and going to college in Peterborough. When I returned from the first Camino, she had struggled with my non-materialistic simple pilgrim approach to life which led to a confrontational relationship that flared up every time we saw each other. What I didn't know at the time was that she was worried about me since my life and work had changed so much. Over the last two years we have come to a better understanding of each other's needs and our relationship has strengthened because of the Camino. Although, I know to this day she still worries about me.

My youngest daughter, Simone, was sixteen and attending high school. More of a free-spirit, she had readily embraced my new-found pilgrim ways when I returned from the Camino. She hadn't questioned my motives and intuitively understood, what was good for me was good for her. She was extremely outgoing and possessed the gregarious qualities of my Dad's personality. We used to do everything together when she lived with me and I really missed her when she chose to move to Peterborough to be with her father. I missed her even more now that I was so far away in Spain. After one ring, my call jumped to their voice mail. Once again, I was disappointed. They were likely on the Internet and it could be hours before they'd be off-line. I left another long, emotional message.

"Hi guys. Too bad you're not there. It's Mum calling from Spain. I really miss you a lot and wanted to talk to you both. I was hoping to catch you before you went to bed. There are lots of students walking the Camino since it's a school holiday this week. I'm reminded of you all day long. I met a lovely boy Marius. I'll tell you all about him when we talk live. Hope you guys are doing well. I'll try to call again in a few days. Know that I love you and miss you lots. Love ya. Bye."

As my voice trailed off, I could feel tears filling my eyes. They all seemed so far away and disconnected from me. I was feeling lonely and discouraged that I couldn't reach them. Next I dialled Bruce's number and waited for the international connection, hopeful when I heard the ringing begin.

"Hello," he answered. As soon as I heard his deep voice, I breathed a sigh of relief.

"Hey Bruce, it's me. How are you?" I asked, relieved that at least we had connected. He was excited to hear from me and had many questions to ask. I talked about the fabulous people I had met and gorgeous countryside. Then I told him about getting mugged, losing my luggage, losing my glasses and all about my horribly blistered feet.

"Sounds like fun," he said dryly. "Wish I was there." I laughed out loud.

"I've walked about forty kilometres so far. It hasn't started off great but I am counting on the Eagle Feather to protect me." Then we talked about his seven-year old daughter Laurel, whom I adored, and he proudly told me all about her progress in school. I asked him to say hello from me and to give her a big hug too. Bruce said he'd received the revisions to the manuscript and it had gone to the publisher to be printed. I was relieved. Then he got more serious.

"You know how much I miss you, Sue," he said followed by a long silent pause, "and since your book is finished, perhaps now you're free to indulge in a romantic relationship?" I knew he was going to bring this up at some point soon but I wasn't sure how to answer it.

"One minute remaining," the recorded operator's voice broke in, "before your call will be disconnected." Now I had to speak quickly.

"I've been thinking a lot about us, but I need this time to walk, to gain more clarity about my purpose and to be with nature. As well, I have to find a recipient for the Eagle Feather and I can't take on anything else right now," I said. He didn't say anything. I knew it sounded like I was making excuses, but I wasn't. I truly believed what I was doing was a step towards furthering my life's vocation and I was committed.

"Okay, do whatever it is you feel you have to do," he said trying to hide his disappointment. "Please be safe and ..." Before anything else could be said, the phone line disconnected. I stood there with my hand on the receiver. Now that there was an ocean between us I longed to be physically close to him. For the first time, I felt a much deeper soulful connection between us. But right now I had my work cut out for me just being a pilgrim on a journey with an Feather.

On the main street, I found a food shop and bought a piece of fish, a fresh-baked baguette and some goat cheese. Back at the albergue, many more pilgrims had arrived. These gregarious spring-time pilgrims were different than the introspective winter pilgrims I'd met on the French Route. They enjoyed themselves as they travelled together with friends and family experiencing the pilgrimage as a group. It seemed to be both a religious and social celebration combined. I dubbed them the Festival Pilgrims.

A little envious of them and missing my family and Bruce, I decided to eat my dinner alone. I cooked the fish in a little olive oil with some sea salt and parsley and sat at a small table. Just as I finished dinner, a solitary pilgrim arrived and introduced himself as Walter, from Poland. He looked to be in his early thirties and was very thin, with long brown wavy hair pulled back into a loose ponytail. He had a calming presence and there was an aura of light that surrounded him which I'd only seen around pilgrims who'd been walking the Camino for several weeks.

Longing to be in his comforting presence, I invited him to join me at the table. Right away, we began speaking as if we had known each other for a lifetime. We shared simple pilgrim stories about life and the virtues of the Camino. In broken English told me he'd walked from Roncesvalles, about 900 kilometres away. He was on his way to another famous pilgrimage site in Fatima, Portugal. He

almost always becomes some kind of a religious or spiritual pilgrimage.

I wondered if someone like Caesar would be a good candidate for the Eagle Feather. He was definitely the leader of the group. He was kind and considerate, but I felt there was something missing. I decided that my decision should speak to me from a place truth. With my hand resting on the Eagle Feather, I promised the Creator that I would honour and listen to my intuition.

We walked further along a dirt path onto a road. We came to a little chapel on the side of the road. Inside there was a statue of Santa Marta, with a very robust and attractive figure. The entire statue was painted a light gold and from a distance, without my glasses, I could see she had something in her hand that looked like a stalk of wheat. On either side of her, there were statues of the Virgin Mary. Here on the Portuguese Route, where Mary is revered, I had noticed that her statues were often set in the middle of the altar with those of Jesus off to one side. In the churches back home, however, the statue of Jesus was almost always in the centre of the altar. I thought about Dino the Greek pilgrim, whom I had met on my previous journey. He told me that a saint is someone who faces their fear. I looked at the angelic face of Santa Marta and wondered what fears she and her stalk of wheat had faced. Even though I was anything but a saint, I also wondered what fears lay before me that I might have to face on this journey.

We left the chapel and returned to the path to walk. Caesar and his friends started to sing an Spanish folk song in Gallego. This is the language spoken in this region of Spain and has Gaelic, Portuguese and Spanish roots. I asked them to teach it to me. They stopped singing, looked at each other, and then laughed out loud. Caesar explained that it wouldn't be suitable for me to sing because it poked fun at the people from this region. I wanted to know more and encouraged him to tell me.

With resistance he loosely translated the words: "I am a Galician … I come from Lugo … I have a bagpipe … where … it's up my butt!" They all roared with laughter. I wasn't impressed since they were mocking the very people who were so generous to me, them, and the other pilgrims. It wasn't a song I wanted to learn and I was sure, without a doubt that Caesar wasn't a candidate for consideration.

We walked for a while, crossed some railway tracks and arrived at the albergue in Pontevedra located next to the train station. Strangely, it was gated and we had to press a buzzer and announce that we were pilgrims in order to gain access. It was a brand new building designed with an open concept. At the registration desk, there was also a store that sold promotional products like T-shirts, hats, rain ponchos, umbrellas and more things with the Camino's logo on them. Because 2004 was a Holy Year there was an increase in the number of pilgrims walking and not a single commercial opportunity had been overlooked.

There was a huge map of the Camino on the wall showing the Portuguese Route with all the albergues listed. Looking at it, Caesar and his friends decided to keep walking another nine kilometres to Balle, Spain, where they would stay for the night. I'd walked twenty kilometres that day and didn't think my knee or the blisters on my feet could handle any more. We exchanged kisses on each cheek and said good-bye.

A friendly hospitalera (a female volunteer who looks after the pilgrims) stamped my credential. She chatted in broken English as she led me to the empty bunkroom where I selected a top bunk in the corner by the window. What a relief! Laying down I closed my eyes for a moment, thinking about how grateful I was to have a bed to sleep in. I sat up and took off my boots and socks to allow my feet to breathe. I unpacked my sleeping bag and rolled it out, took the bandages off my feet and then had a hot shower. I changed into my pilgrim pyjamas—fresh underwear and a clean micro-fibre vest—and crawled into my sleeping bag. Even though it was only 5:00 p.m. and I was hungry, I fell fast asleep.

The sound of Spanish and Portuguese being spoken loudly all around, woke me up. Only a half-hour had passed while I slept, yet every bunk was filled with pilgrims who all seemed to know each other. Since I couldn't sleep, I got up and decided to take a walk around the city. I found a place called A Peregrina Square and went into the sanctuary of Virxe Peregrina, a fascinating Baroque-style Cathedral built in 1778. Its floor plan was impressively shaped in the form of a scallop shell. Imagine building an entire Cathedral dedicated to *Las Peregrinas*—the women who walk!

Inside the eighteenth century building, a large statue of the Madre Maria stood in the center of the altar, with suspended angel cherubs flying all around her. Rows of candles flickered along one wall. I went over, said a short prayer and then I lit a candle for the women in my life: my children, my Mum, my grandmother, my sisters, my mother-in-law, my sisters-in-law, and my girlfriends. Leaving by the vestibule, I dropped two Euros in the donation box and picked up a prayer card with the Madre Maria's benevolent image on it to give to my Mother when I got home. I saw a poster that said an Easter celebration was taking place that night at the Cathedral from 9:00 p.m. to 2:00 a.m. but unfortunately the albergue curfew was 9:30 p.m. so I wouldn't be joining in the festivities.

When I got back, the albergue was overflowing with pilgrims. There were mattresses spread out on the floor in the bunkroom, hall and kitchen. I bought hot chocolate from a vending machine and sat on the sofa in the main room. With my feet soaking in a ceramic basin, I began writing in my diary. Two lively young men appeared at the door laughing out loud. They looked around the room.

"*Buenos,*" I said with my poor Spanish accent.

"*Buenos*," they said and then introduced themselves as pilgrims from Spain. One of them, Alberto had blue eyes and light brown hair. The other, Santiago, had dark brown eyes and black hair. They told me it was their first day of walking the Camino and they were looking for somewhere to sleep. The hostel was completely full and most of the available floor space was taken up by pilgrims. I assured both of them that I had a bunk bed already and they were welcome to use the sofa. I quickly dried my feet and said goodnight.

After brushing my teeth, I changed for bed. I checked out the blister on my right foot to see that it was red and inflamed. I massaged both feet with olive oil, did some healing Reiki treatment, put on clean socks and quietly went to bed. I had a fitful sleep until the unending snoring of the other pilgrims finally woke me up.

12

The Women Who Serve

Outside the albergue in Pontevedra, a group of pilgrims I recognized from the path stood by the wall of the sanctuary of the Virxe Peregrina church. I waved and one of them pointed down the street. A religious procession was approaching, led by a priest and two altar boys carrying tall candles on wooden staves. A crowd of about seventy people followed them. When they got closer, I realized they were all women well-dressed in fur coats and stylish leather shoes.

Following behind them, six men in long brown robes who looked like monks were pushing a large float through the narrow street. It was covered with a green velvet drape and I assumed it held a massive statue that looked to be about three metres high. With great difficulty, they struggled to move the large float uphill, past the women who'd parted to either side of the street. A priest dressed in a white gown sang out the words of a prayer. The women repeated the words back to him in song. They looked very solemn and some of them were even crying.

Inexplicably, I felt their emotion and despite not knowing all of the details of this sacred ceremony, I started crying in sympathetic sorrow, too. When the prayer was over, the crowd dispersed, many of them returning to the church. I dried my eyes and left as well. Alone again, I started to walk back towards the church and then habitually followed the yellow arrows out of the city. As soon as I saw a stone, I picked it up and carried it with me. I felt particularly strong that morning. The Camino took me into a luscious chestnut grove where birds were singing non-stop. I loved being in the forest, feeling protected by the trees. While in the stillness of Mother Earth, I thought the Eagle Feather would appreciate being here. I set my backpack down and took it out of the deerskin pouch I'd kept in my inside coat pocket. Opening the red cloth I gently lifted it out of its home, while talking to it like it was a baby of mine. With my arms stretched out, unsure which direction was east, I held it up to the trees, surrendered myself and spoke in a loud voice, "*Miigwech Creator*," I called out with reverence. I touched the Eagle Feather to my chest and held it close to my heart in a moment of silent prayer. A bird flew by. Instead of putting it back in the inside pocket of my coat, I wanted to feel it connected closer to my body. Wrapping it ritualistically in the red cloth, I slipped it into the cotton belt around my waist that held my passport and money. It fit snugly and safely below the waistband of my pants, resting over my *hara*—located just below my navel. The hara is the body's central source of *chi* energy; the place the Japanese refer to as the body's point of balance. By placing it there, it was connecting my highest energy to the Creator. I felt at peace.

After an hour or so, I passed through a stand of pine and eucalyptus trees where I stopped at the side of the path to rest. My feet felt better than they had the day before and I had hoped that they were finally healing. Looking upward, I could now see dark clouds rolling in. Pilgrims I had met said the south of Spain was getting torrential rain and snow but in the north, it had been beautiful sunny weather for five days, which was very unusual for the region of Galicia in the spring. I tried not to think about the difficulties I might encounter if I was walking for hours in the rain. Instead I listened closely to the sound of moving water from the stream weaving through the thick woods. My body and spirit were balanced and I was finally feeling at ease.

The route meandered under the forest canopy. I looked for the yellow arrow signs, but I couldn't see any so I just followed the clearly-defined path. Once out of the forest the luscious and rolling Galician countryside presented itself to me like a gift. It started to rain but I just kept walking, letting it fall on me as though it was washing me. At home, I would run for cover if it rained, but on the Camino there wasn't anywhere to go. There were no buildings or trees for shelter so I embraced it. Fortunately, the rain only lasted for about ten minutes.

For about two kilometres the path was covered with large loose rocks about the size of tennis balls making it tricky to balance my weight. Despite being awkward to walk over now, I knew they would be appreciated by future pilgrims when the path was a mass of thick mud from the torrential rain usually experienced in this region. Surrounded by this path of stones, I made it a point to find a small one for each of my daughters and I put their sorrow into them. While setting the last one down, I noticed a piece of crystal glittering in the sunlight amongst the other gray stones. I picked it up and began to rub it, tapping into its healing properties. Immediately, I opened myself to connect with the love of the entire universe. At first I felt in a state of harmony but then without any warning, I became very solemn. A grave sense of sadness overcame me and I started to cry, reacting as though there had been a death. Still rubbing the crystal between my fingers and thinking of my daughters, it became clear to me that it was the death of my marriage to their father that I was grieving. Crying openly, I held the stone while I walked with the intention of forgiving both myself and John. Finally giving myself permission to release the emotion from my body, I set the crystal stone down on the path, leaving all my sorrow behind.

Arriving in the city of Caldas de Reis, I followed the signs directing me to the Cathedral and found a newly renovated, sixteenth century albergue next door. It had gray marble floors which gleamed in the sunlit main lobby and an ornate banister that led upstairs. The hospitalero (a male volunteer who cares for the pilgrims) registered me and stamped my passport. He assigned me to a room—*numero uno*—and when I entered it two older couples were already there. We greeted each other warmly, but that was the extent of our spoken conversation. I found out they didn't speak a word of English so there was a lot of smiling, nodding and pointing after that. In the kitchen I found a bucket and filled it with my blister potion: warm water, vinegar and sea salt. New blisters had appeared on my baby toes and while I was hunched over examining them closely, I heard familiar laughter and then a man's voice said, "*Hola, peregrina.*"

It was Alberto, the young handsome, blue-eyed Spanish pilgrim I'd met in Pontevedra. He waved from across the room.

"Hey, Alberto. How's it going?" I asked. He walked over to where I was sitting and invited me to go with him to a café down the street where he was meeting his friend, Santiago. Craving some conversation and light-hearted fun, I dried my feet, put on my boots and we left.

At the café, Santiago, the more sombre of the two, was also thrilled in his own way to see me. They both asked lots of questions about my life, especially about my three daughters. Alberto told me he was twenty-three years old and wanted to be a famous movie star. A friend of his was producing an independent film and he was very excited about his speaking role in it. I told them about receiving the Eagle Feather from my friend Sherry and shared what I knew about its significance in Native folklore. Alberto said he should receive it. He felt he was truly an eagle in spirit. The music in the cafe was loud and very soon I grew tired of it and I left them to go back to my room.

As I sat on the bunk bed quietly writing in my diary, the two older couples came into the room. They greeted me and then continued laughing loudly. The men looked like they had enjoyed a little too much red wine. I watched as the women made up the beds for them by laying out their sleeping bags. The men sat down at the edge of the bed, while the women continued talking, kneeling in front of them while taking off their shoes and socks. Then their wives began undressing them, as though they were children. I laughed to myself and tried not to stare but I was fascinated by the oddly intimate domestic scene that was unfolding in front of me.

The women washed their husbands' bare feet, then rubbed them with foot lotion and put their socks back on for them. They told the men to rollover, which they did with laughter and great difficulty because of their large, protruding stomachs. The women massaged their backs with ointment while the men moaned in delight. Then they tucked and zipped them into their sleeping bags, finishing the ritual off with a quick kiss on the lips.

The full-bodied women, now giggling and talking back and forth loudly in Spanish, like young girls at a pyjama party, began the difficult task of climbing into the top bunks without a ladder. One woman stood on the lower bunk and tried to lift her chunky leg onto the top mattress to pull her self up, while the other woman pushed her from behind. Smiling to myself, I thought this was like watching two sea lions crawl onto a rock. They both managed to clamber up while laughing with delight. Once on the top bunk they put on their own pyjamas and then rubbed each other's feet before going to sleep themselves. Although they obviously had very traditional husband and wife roles, I observed that the two women had served the men, and each other, with unconditional love, kindness and honour. I admired them for their dedication to serving and the fact that they all had so much fun, too. Most of my married life, John and I had concentrated our efforts on establishing equal roles because neither of us believed that only women should serve in the household. That night I really considered, who was I to judge whether their defined gender roles were right or wrong? They gave me a different perspective on serving. When I finished writing about them in my diary, I got up and turned out the light. Before closing my eyes to go to sleep, I paused. Could I humble myself enough to wash someone's feet in an act of pure selfless serving? Was I a woman who served?

13

Nearing the Half-way Point

I awoke to the sound of zippers being zipped on sleeping bags and the bustle of pilgrims getting ready to walk. It was Good Friday and I was in Caldas de Reis. Since there was only one bathroom for the women, there was a line up. Instead of waiting, I went downstairs. Someone had left a large loaf of Galician raisin bread on the kitchen counter, so I helped myself. I drank as much water as I could and then returned to use the bathroom. I checked the pilgrim guide and discovered that I had roughly twenty kilometres to reach the city of Padron. Feeling optimistic and strong, I swung my backpack over my shoulders and left through the same door I came in. Outside I was greeted by an all-male marching band that was on the street in front of the Church of Saint Tomas. The men, in black suits and white shirts, were warming up their instruments. A crowd of people, young and old, stood waiting and so I also lingered, to see what was about to happen.

It was the start of another religious procession, this time with two men carrying a glass casket decorated with gold. Inside was an effigy of Jesus Christ, complete with dark red blood running out of his wounded heart. About ten metres behind them, another group of men carried a platform with a beautiful statue of a sorrowful Mother Mary dressed in black velvet with gold trim. I wondered if they were the same statues I'd seen the day before which had been draped in the green velvet cloth. The band followed behind playing a solemn hymn that I vaguely recognized from my Catholic upbringing. Everyone sang while carrying a lit candle, following the procession through the narrow streets.

After they passed, I found myself standing beside a fountain. Two streams of very hot water spurted out of the side of a wall and into a small cistern. A plaque, dated 1882, said that this was the site of a Roman bath. Pilgrims often stopped here to be healed of their ailments so I took off my boots and socks, anxious to test the miraculous waters. One foot at a time, I cautiously slipped my feet into the steaming hot water, hoping this would help heal my blisters. After only a few minutes, I quickly removed my reddened feet and put my socks and boots back on. Feeling invigorated, I got up and began my journey once again.

Back on the road, I heard my name being called from behind and turned around. It was Alberto and Santiago again. Alberto playfully winked as he approached, but Santiago was concerned about my knee. There was a gentle giant-like quality to him that matched his strong Spanish features. He suggested that I try his anti-inflammatory spray and generously insisted that he carry my backpack as well as his own. He said that serving others was the spirit of the Camino. "On the Camino we should help each other whenever we can." I was honoured. Then Santiago unexpectedly left the path and went into the forest alone. He returned moments later and presented me with a sturdy walking stick that he'd found for me on the forest floor. I was amazed at the maturity of this young man who wasn't more than twenty-five years old. Thanking him, I thought about how Sherry had said the recipient would acknowledge me with love, kindness and honour. I was beginning to associate the act of serving, as a pilgrim virtue that aligned with the qualities of the person who would receive the Eagle Feather.

Santiago decided to walk ahead, so I joined Alberto who was bopping along to music on his CD player. He asked me if I still had the Eagle Feather and I assured him that I hadn't given it away yet. This seemed to please him. To distract me from my sore knee, he urged me to listen to the song that was playing. I didn't see the point in listening to music on the Camino, since I preferred the sounds of nature. Reluctantly I took the ear plugs and I was surprised to find that it distracted me from my pain. Soon we stopped at a store and I bought some chocolate to share with them. This time, Alberto graciously took a turn at serving and carried my backpack.

Early in the afternoon we arrived in the city of Padron. This is the coastal city where the ship carrying the body of Saint James landed after travelling from Palestine in 44 AD with some of his disciples. There was a steeple in the distance so I knew we were close to the next albergue. Waiting for us to catch up to him, Santiago pointed out a gorgeous statue of Rosina de Castro, a famous Spanish poet.

We climbed a steep cobblestone hill, past the eighteenth century Carmelite Convent of O Carme. True to form, the albergue was beside the church, in a historic building that had been stunningly renovated. It was late in the afternoon when we arrived. A handful of pilgrims were lined up at a desk and a young woman was registering them. When it was my turn, she asked for my pilgrim credential, then noted my age, my reason for walking and my mode of transportation. Walking upstairs to the bunk room, I noticed the stone walls of the albergue were at least half a metre thick. The floors were made of thick pine boards with a high-gloss finish and were clean enough to eat off. The wooden ceiling was stained in a rich cherry tone. The bunk beds were painted dark green and each had a cream coloured wool blanket neatly folded at the end. I selected a bunk near a window with green shutters. Wrought iron latches held the two windows closed and when I released them, the windows swung open letting a gentle mountain breeze into the room. Below, was a quilted patchwork of farmland—creating a truly sumptuous vista.

I went downstairs to check out the kitchen and facilities. The walls of the room were stone. There was a handsome fireplace that must have once been used for cooking. Its chimney was still there, but now it hovered over an efficiently designed, built-in stovetop and counter. Off the kitchen, there was a separate private room with four single beds and a washroom, perhaps set aside for pilgrims who were handicapped, injured or sick. Alberto and Santiago came into the room and announced that we had an invitation for dinner with a Spanish couple who had traveled from San Sebastian by train and then walked from Tui, Spain. The woman, Ana, had helped Santiago with his injured knee.

We agreed to go shopping to buy something to contribute for dinner. Outside, we crossed the stone bridge again and stopped at a farmer's cart on the street where a village woman sold home-made bread, and an aptly-named breast-shaped cheese, modelled by hand, called *Tetilla*. We bought a selection of bread and cheese and returned to the kitchen. We offered to help but Ana and her husband assured us that they wanted to serve us dinner. Sitting at a long wooden table with a bench on each side, we talked with them and snacked on local cornbread with raisins and some of the cheese. Alberto had fun playing with the *Tetilla* cheese. He held it up to his chest and everyone laughed at him. Ana's husband prepared a rice salad while she made a *tortilla*.

Dinner was served and a prayer of grace was said by the couple in Spanish. Since it was Good Friday, we didn't eat meat. It was typical Spanish fare: *tortilla y patata* (spicy fried potato pancakes) fresh tuna salad, rice with vegetables, bread and cheese. A large group of people at the other table began singing folk songs and soon everyone in the room joined them. There were families and friends of many different ages who obviously enjoyed walking the Camino together. They made a point of including me in their celebrations as though I was a part of their family and I was truly grateful for their hospitality and care. When dinner was finished, everyone joined in and did the dishes together. It was a perfect evening together.

Back upstairs in the bunkroom, I laid down on the hard wooden floor to stretch my back and reviewed my plans for the next day. There were only twenty-three kilometers left to walk to Santiago. My plan was to spend one night there and then continue westerly for another ninety kilometres to Cabo Finisterre, almost the half-way point. From there I would follow the last stretch of the Camino north to Muxia where I would turn around and walk the reverse route, roughly 230 kilometres, to end up back where I had started in Portugal.

Nearing the mid-point of my journey I thought about the words of my rowing coach, Peter Cookson, who used to say that the half-way point is where the race actually begins. Over time, I learned to trust that, if I put my energy into preparing for the first half of the race, it would mentally set me up for success in the second half. This approach strengthened my race and I decided to apply this strategy to my life. Since my maternal grandmother Daisy Hirst, lived to be ninety-six years old, I've always believed that I will live to be at least 100. Since I was almost fifty years of age, I figured my life race was only just beginning. The possibilities to create in the second half of my life, were endless.

It had gotten so cold in the room that I got up and crawled into my sleeping bag. Alberto had come upstairs as well and he was standing by the open window. His slender body was silhouetted against the moonlit sky. Slouched in a James Dean pose, he was smoking a cigarette. He took a long drag on the cigarette and then exhaled, sending a series of smoke rings floating in my direction.

What he didn't know was that I am hypo-allergic to cigarette smoke. A mild breeze carried the smoke directly to me and I began to cough uncontrollably. I pulled the sleeping bag over my head and I quickly went to sleep. If his aim was to impress me, it obviously didn't work.

14

Returning to Santiago

On my first Camino, I learned a pilgrim aphorism that I have never forgotten: If you walk past a pilgrim in need, you must go back to the beginning of your journey and walk it all over again. Since I was back walking the Camino a second time, I wondered if I had literally or figuratively walked past a pilgrim in need, if not on the Camino, then at some other point in my life.

It was 5:30 a.m. on Easter Sunday and I was again soaking my feet. Alberto and Santiago entered with their backpacks on. Apologetically, Santiago said they were leaving early that morning so they could arrive at the Cathedral in Santiago by mid-day, since they both had to be at work on Monday. He seemed genuinely uneasy about leaving without me, although I couldn't help wonder if they wanted to shed the burden of an injured pilgrim.

After soaking my feet, I carefully placed the gel-like blister patches and medical tape over the open sores, then slathered my feet in Vaseline and put on clean socks. Gathering my things together, I packed and left, even though it was still dark outside. I wandered around the streets looking for a yellow arrow but without a flashlight, I couldn't find a single one.

When I was just about to give up and return to the albergue, I saw a light moving back and forth behind me. It was a flashlight and belonged to a short, stout man. He was leading a large tour group of Festival Pilgrims and when he saw me alone, he invited me to join them. I accepted and started walking along the dirt road with them. We passed some new homes and then came to a dead end. He was obviously annoyed at the situation and got everyone's attention by yelling at the top of his lungs in Gallego. Swinging his arm in the air, he turned them around in the opposite direction. Comically, everyone obediently followed his orders without question; myself included.

He led us along the side of the highway to another section of the Camino path that veered off the road. We followed it and ended up back on the same highway again. Frustrated, he charged ahead of the group, marching with a sense of purpose as the cars raced past us at one hundred and twenty kilometres per hour. We came to a restaurant and he decided everyone would stop for a break. Since I wanted to keep walking, I thanked him for his guidance and we waved goodbye.

The warmth of the rising sun reminded me of the advice of Sherry's grandmother. Sunrise was the best time to pray to the Creator. I stopped, turned to the east and set my pack down on the gravel that filled the shoulder of the road. Taking the red cloth package from my money belt, I carefully untied it, opened the fabric and tucked it in my pocket. While I did this, I found myself talking to the Eagle Feather, thanking it for caring for me I assured it that I would find a worthy recipient. Since we had walked the path together for several days now, I was feeling closer to it, almost like we were getting to know each other more intimately. I held the Eagle Feather up to the sun.

"Miigwech Creator," I said. I bowed my head and added a simple prayer of thanks. Just as I finished, the morning sun rose over the horizon, blessing the beginning of a new day. I returned the Eagle Feather to its home and began walking the Camino path again.

Even though today was Easter Sunday, no one seemed to talk about the Easter Bunny. Spaniards take their Catholic feast days very seriously. In all of the villages I passed through, people were preparing special meals, and busy planning religious ceremonies and festivities with their family and friends. Although my journey wasn't planned to coincide with this celebration, I was being re-introduced to some of the traditions of my Catholic upbringing and for the first time in a very long time, I wasn't resisting them.

My pace had slowed considerably. Many other pilgrims easily strode past me. I was tired of thinking the same thoughts over again and again. The rising and falling path wound through the Spanish villages where the stone houses, were adorned with red tile roofs. By noon, I entered a forested area where I sat down on the edge of the path to have a snack. A tall German pilgrim approached and introduced himself by his nickname, Kiko. I invited him to rest with me. He said he recognized me from the Easter procession in Pontevedra. He told me he was originally from Berlin and not surprisingly, like most Germans, he spoke perfect English. He'd moved to Spain several years ago because he loved the country and the people. He kindly invited me to join him and his group of Spanish friends up ahead and so I did. There were two men and two women; one of whom had dyed a bright red streak down the middle of her jet black hair.

Nearing out destination, the group decided to stop at a restaurant just inside Santiago's city limits. I wondered if they were purposely delaying their arrival to the holy city. It reminded me of how I felt when I had entered Santiago the first time. On the last day Andreas and I had walked very slowly, neither of us wanting the Camino to end. At the time, I naively told Andreas that when the Camino ended, the journey was just beginning. I only discovered how powerful those words truly were when I finally returned home. Instead of returning to the familiarity and security of a job in the corporate world, I embarked on a brand new life journey by using my voice to create new possibilities to live my higher purpose to inspire people.

I bought some canned sardines, crackers, a chocolate bar, yogurt and orange juice and then sat down with the others. Kiko treated all of us to *cafe con leche*. The conversation was lively and energized. I took my boots off and so did the woman sitting next to me with the red streak in her hair. She also had blisters on the heels and bottom of her feet covered with bandages. Grinning at me, she pulled two maxi-sized sanitary napkins out of her pack and then shoved them inside her boots. She looked up, saw me watching her and then we both laughed out loud together. She slipped her feet on top of them and made a face to show how comfortable they were.

She offered me a pair and I pressed them into my boots, too. We laughed again. I couldn't believe it. They were perfect blister cushions for a size-nine boot and obviously absorbed moisture too. I wished I could have had a conversation with this clever woman. She was resourceful and obviously had a great sense of humour, too. Perhaps she was a potential candidate for the Eagle Feather, but I realized I had no way of making that decision. She didn't speak English and my Spanish was *poco* at best. Considering how much explaining I would have to do, for the first time I wondered if maybe the recipient of the Eagle Feather would have to speak English.

We left as a group and began the final stage of our walk to Santiago. Gasping for air, we struggled up the steep incline. Although it was a difficult climb, I loved the challenge of being physically pushed to my limits. My thigh muscles were burning and my breathing was fast and laboured. From training in the sport of rowing, I had discovered that the stronger my body was physically, the stronger my mind was mentally. Repeating the word Camino as a mantra, helped me to stay focussed. Finally, we reached the summit, which was the highest point in that region according to Kiko. We walked along the narrow path that wound its way across the edge of the mountain where we could see the city of Santiago. The towers of the Cathedral in the old quarter stood above all the other buildings. Seeing it again, from this perspective, gave me an overwhelming feeling of joy. I put my hand the Eagle Feather and thanked it for being a part of my journey.

It was downhill from here and that meant the toughest part of the day's journey lay ahead of us. We walked in single file following Kiko's lead and soon came to a set of railroad tracks. We ducked through an opening in the security fence and walked across several sets of train tracks until we reached the other side. The narrow dirt path continued down a steep embankment before finally reaching the outskirts of the bustling city of Santiago. We walked through a residential area. There were lots of birds singing and flying around us. We trekked into a busy commercial area, past office buildings and retail shops—surrounded by the noisy, smelly, jangling sounds of urban life. The confusion of walking through the busy city streets baffled all of us and as a result even Kiko had trouble finding the yellow arrows. Already, I longed to be back in the serene forest embraced in the living womb of Mother Nature. The streets narrowed as we approached the older section of the historical city. Right away I noticed brass scallop shells imbedded into the sidewalks guiding the way and I felt comforted by their presence.

Boisterous crowds filled the streets and every store was packed with customers. The windows of the restaurants displayed fresh pulpo, calamari, mussels, clams and large selections of fish. In the doorways of the souvenir shops, young women carrying trays of desserts called out to the pilgrims to try a free sample of Santiago Torte, a flan-like cake that's a specialty of the region. To the Spanish, Easter Sunday is the most important religious event of the year, even more important than Christmas, and today everyone was celebrating. Kiko and the other men stopped and went into one of the souvenir shops. The women and I kept walking even though the crowds of people filling the streets made it more difficult for our group to stay together.

Soon, the men caught up to us wearing silly brown felt pilgrim's hats that they had purchased. The front brim was pulled up and fastened with a white plastic scallop shell. The women laughed at them and I found myself judging them. I thought the hats looked ridiculous and I was surprised that they would resort to such mockery of pilgrims. Any ideas I had about Kiko being the recipient of the Eagle Feather vanished at that moment. I began to wonder how could I possibly find someone who would fit the rigorous criteria? I placed my hand over the Eagle Feather and opening my heart, I asked the Creator to help me face my fears.

Kiko said they were going to a bar and invited me to join them but I wanted to be alone for the final steps and I soon lost them in the crowds. My mind became very focussed. Putting one foot in front of the other, I walked in complete surrender with the hope that somehow I was completing a circle in my life. I had returned to the place where I had once ended a journey. Without effort I was being carried along.

15

Sacred Steps

Following the cobblestone road that wound its way through the old city, my mind was locked on arriving to the Cathedral. I placed my hand over the Eagle Feather, as I walked past the ancient stone buildings. I turned a corner and Obradoiro Square opened up in front of me. Overwhelmed by its magnificence I walked slowly towards the main doors of one of the ancient landmarks of Christendom; the Cathedral of Saint James. Standing outside the immense doors leading into the Portico de la Gloria, I was once again stunned by its magnificent artistic beauty. My head tilted back to take in the soaring, luminous glory of all that I saw before me. There were no words to describe it, only a feeling of immense hope.

There was a special entrance to the cathedral called the Puerta Santa or more commonly, the Holy Door which is only opened during a Holy Year. I joined a short line-up outside the ornate iron gates and walked through the door entering the Cathedral as a pilgrim for the second time in my life. This time, though, I had the honour of bearing a sacred Eagle Feather. Unfortunately, I had just missed the pilgrim Mass which had started at noon, but the Cathedral was still filled with tourists and pilgrims from all over the world. Sunlight glinted off the gold façade behind the altar, bathing the famous statue of Saint James the Apostle in a light of divine softness. The Apostle's remains were held sacrosanct in a tomb below the altar. I walked up the centre aisle drawn toward the famous statue, supremely grateful that the Camino had guided me here again. Tears filled my eyes. I blessed myself in front of the altar, turned to the left and slid into an empty pew at the front. I set my pack down and pulled the kneeler forward. I knelt and automatically began to recite the Hail Mary a number of times. When I finished I just spoke to God in my own words, saying a simple prayer of thanks.

I looked at my watch and it was almost 2:00 p.m., the exact time I had scheduled to meet Judith at her hotel. I decided to complete the other pilgrim rituals after meeting her for lunch. I went outside and walked across Obradoiro Square to the famous Parador Hostal de los Reyes Catolicos; an elegant fifteenth century building that was once a hospital for pilgrims. The owners of the hotel still maintained a historical obligation to provide a free breakfast, lunch and dinner for up to ten pilgrims daily. Inside the main lobby, I asked the concierge to let Judith know I'd arrived and took a seat on an ornate velvet sofa, worrying just a little that my dirty clothes would mark the fabric. Sitting there, patient and still, I was transported back to the magical time when I had arrived there before with Andreas. It was a cold December day. We were fresh off the Camino path and life held all the possibilities one could imagine. Moments later, my reverie ended when a striking red-headed woman, who could only be Judith approached.

"Are you Sue Kenney?"

"Yes," I said standing up. "You must be Judith." She gave me a gentle hug and the becoming scent of her perfume enveloped me.

"What a fine pilgrim you are," she said, standing back, looking me over. "I am so happy to meet you."

"And I'm thrilled to meet you, too. Thanks for your generous offer to go for lunch," I said excitedly.

"Come, come," she said, "we must go to my room so you can enjoy a nice hot shower before we go out to eat."

Judith was a very attractive and poised woman. She wore a long navy blue wool skirt, a crisp white shirt with a lime green shawl over her shoulders. Her thick red hair was held back with a black hair-band and she had a warm smile. I knew for certain that I didn't smell as nice as she did. She called the porter over and he picked up my backpack. We followed him past the wrought-iron gate, across the courtyard and through a huge carved wooden door. We got on the elevator and went up one floor. It felt strange to be served this way.

When she opened the door to her room, I had another overpowering flashback of Andreas at this same hotel. When we arrived there, I had been so excited about not sleeping in a bunk bed again, that I ran into the room and jumped up on the enormous bed falling on my back. This time when I saw the bed, I managed to contain my excitement. The porter set down my backpack and Judith immediately showed me to the bathroom.

"Take your time and help yourself to anything you need," she said kindly and closed the door.

After stripping off all my clothes, I walked past a full-length mirror and stopped to study the pilgrim reflected in front of me. My body had become more muscular and slimmer. There was a lot of colour in my face. I liked what I saw. I turned on the bathtub taps, delighted to find there was unlimited hot water and lots of pressure. Leaving the bandages on my feet, I stepped into the shower and stood there, unable to move as a flood of warm water washed over my body.

Again my mind went back in time to the memories of my first Camino where I'd spent time every day practicing the art of self-love. I believed that if every thought, action, intention and emotion came from love, then I could live my life from this place and I couldn't go wrong. The practise of self-love hadn't really been tested until one day Andreas and I were climbing the mountain of

Cebreiro. Every so often, we'd stop to admire the beauty of the mighty mountains. I would stand with my heart completely open and surrender myself to accepting all the love of the universe. It was during one of those moments, I suddenly felt an overwhelming force of energy move into every cell in my body. It was as though a feeling of universal love had enraptured my entire body, igniting a fire within me. I wasn't ready to accept it and quickly passed the love along to Andreas, who was standing beside me. Then I turned back to the mountain and again surrendered myself to receiving. This time, the love returned but even stronger and my knees buckled. Pausing, for a moment, I considered whether to send the love away again or keep it. In a split second I made the decision to give myself permission to receive absolute love. I remember standing there motionless, in a state of love. I let its powerful radiance fill me. Aware that something special taken place, Andreas asked me what had happened. I described the moment to him clarifying that in the past, whenever I gave my love away, most people would keep it. When I asked him why he didn't keep all the love I gave him, in a calm caring voice he said, "It wasn't mine to keep."

Because Andreas permitted the love to flow back to the mountain and return to me again that day, I discovered that giving and receiving love wasn't only way for me to live from a place of love. I could *be* love in every thought, action, emotion and intention from anywhere. It was during that life-altering moment, Andreas and I had fallen deeply in love. Five days later, we finally arrived in Santiago together and physically celebrated the union of our souls, right here at the Parador Hotel.

Suddenly my mind snapped into the present moment, as the hot water soothed my body. I stepped out of the shower and wrapped the huge white fluffy towel around me as if trying to hold onto the memories I had from that night, long ago. I got dressed and walked out of the bathroom fresh and clean, but in my worn, filthy clothes again.

"Shall we go for lunch now?" Judith asked unaware of my state of mind. I looked up at her with a smile, hiding my disappointment that she wasn't Andreas.

"Yes, I'm ready," I said excitedly. "Let's go."

I placed the Eagle Feather into my backpack and left it in Judith's the room, just in case we were going to have wine with our meal. As we walked down the hall, and into the elevator, it felt strange to be without both my pack and the beloved Eagle Feather. We chatted while walking through the courtyard and I asked where we were eating lunch. Judith pointed to the formal dining room of the hotel—where Andreas and I had eaten the first night we stayed together. Again I asked myself why I was returning to all of the same places to re-live the special moments, but this time without Andreas?

Judith ordered creamy yellow caviar and pressed pulpo—followed by salad. For the main course we both had sea bass served with thinly sliced potatoes and shared a bottle of local Galician white wine.

"I want to give you a gift," Judith said with anticipation. "it is something light enough to carry." She set three stones in front of me. They were light pink and in the shape of a flower. "They are Oklahoma Rose Stones." Judith said proudly, pointing to the stones. "Choose which one you want Sue, or take them all." I looked closely at each stone.

"I've been told that Native people believe that we don't choose the stones, the stones choose us," I said picking up the one that I thought chose me. I rubbed it between my fingers and thanked Judith. Then I offered her one of the stones I brought from home and shared my Sorrow Stone story with her. She listened closely as I proceeded to tell her the simple fable Andreas had passed on to me.

The same one that I had told Marius, the young Spanish boy I'd met earlier in my journey. It was the reactions that I got from telling this story, both in person and in my first book, that helped convince me that sharing stories of the Camino was part of my actual life purpose.

Even though she wasn't a Catholic, Judith said she loved the Camino. She was raised Pentecostal—and yet had been to Santiago four times. She had actually walked it twice, both the entire Portuguese Route and part of the French Route. At first she struck me as a very serious person but I soon learned that she had a great sense of humour.

"Once in Santiago," she said, "I went to Confession and asked a priest to pray for a dear friend of mine who'd just been diagnosed with cancer. The priest offered me a list of sins that I could choose from and I picked a couple of minor ones that seemed most appropriate." I put my hand over my mouth holding back the laughter. "So I went to Confession for the first time, and then called my friend and happily informed her there was a two-for-one sin sale in Santiago." We both laughed out loud. Since that day, she had vowed to go to Confession, at least once every year, for the rest of her life.

Judith's story reminded me that unlike her, I never wanted to go to Confession, ever again in my life. Even though I was told a pilgrim earns plenary indulgences by completing the rituals of walking the Camino, attending Mass at the Cathedral, receiving Holy Communion, and by going to Confession. During the Holy Year, if a pilgrim also walked through the Holy Door, they would be entitled to receive absolution from eternal damnation for their entire life. This was a tempting offer for a lapsed Catholic like me, but I understood it meant that I'd have to go through the formal procedure of going to a priest for Confession. Thinking about it reminded me of what I would have to do. Once I stepped into the dark wooden booth, then I'd kneel down with my hands in a prayer position and the priest would slide open the wooden cover to reveal a screen that barely disguised my identity. With my head bowed down, I would have to say the words: "Bless me Father for I have sinned. It has been almost 30 years since my last confession and these are my sins." Just the thought of doing this in my mind confirmed there was no way I was going through it. Instead I would rely on my ongoing personal relationship with God for reconciliation and pass on life-time absolution.

We enjoyed fresh-baked apple crepes for dessert and had a *cafe solo* that finished the meal perfectly. I must admit, although feeling a little guilty about the un-pilgrim-like extravagances, I really enjoyed the food, service and exquisite surroundings. We left to walk around the old city together. I hadn't arranged for a place to stay that night and had planned to walk to the Seminary hostel about a kilometre away. Judith insisted that was too far for me to walk. She offered to help me find something closer and while I sat at a café with my blistered feet raised up on a chair, she went to the Santiago Tourist Office to get a list of accommodations.

A half-hour later she returned to say that there were very few rooms available in the city because it was Easter weekend but she had found a room for me, only a few hundred metres away. She had once stayed there when she was a pilgrim. The owner of the hostel had offered her the last bed he had available for that night and at fifteen Euros, the price was perfect. She walked with me to the hostel and we climbed a set of wide stairs. It was dark and dingy. At the top of the stairs a bald man appeared and invited us in with a welcoming smile. He showed us a small, messy room with a single bed in front of a curtain that was slightly open, displaying rows of shelves lined with folded sheets, blankets and pillows.

On one wall, there was an ironing board with linens piled on it. Along another wall, a long wooden table was covered with paper and stacks of files. The room had a high ceiling, making it appear larger than it really was. It was really more like a glorified storage closet. He took us down the hall where there was a clean bathroom with a white porcelain claw-foot bathtub—the only thing that sold me on staying there. It certainly wasn't the Parador Hotel, but when he also assured me that there was lots of hot water, I agreed to take it.

The owner said he was going to a store and asked if I needed anything. Gratefully, I asked him to bring me some vinegar and sea salt. While he was gone, Judith kindly helped me unpack and get the room ready for the evening. When he returned with the supplies, he refused to take any money from me. He said it was a gift. He handed Judith an empty bucket and told her to fill it with warm water from the bathroom. The owner placed a white towel on a chair and then left.

Judith lugged the bucket back to where I was sitting and added the vinegar and sea salt. With care, she helped me slip my feet into the familiar pungent solution and then sat down on the armless wooden chair, in the middle of the room. Hunched over, resting her elbows with the folded towel on her lap, she swished the water around my feet. We talked intimately about the basic needs of being a simple Camino pilgrim. Judith used the clean towel and helped dry my feet. I put on my socks and boots. I thought about the two Spanish women I had seen at the albergue caring for their husband's feet, realizing what a great honour it was to be served this way. Through her actions Judith had served me with love, kindness and honour. She was a true pilgrim, although, I was sure even if I offered her the Eagle Feather, she wouldn't accept it.

It was around 6:00 p.m. and Judith said she had to get back to the hotel to pack, as she was catching a 4:00 a.m. taxi to the airport the next day. My plan was to go to the Cathedral and complete the rituals of the pilgrims of old, minus Confession, of course. She accompanied me to the Pilgrim Office to get my credential stamped and receive my Compostela. There was a short line-up that ended at the bottom of the stairs where we said an emotional good-bye. Watching her walk away into the crowd, I saw an image of her sitting on the old wooden chair beside my bed, helping me to care for my feet. It occurred to me that it was during this holy celebration that Jesus washed the feet of his disciples, as an act of serving and the honour of being served. Resting on the chair in the simple room, Judith had looked so comfortable, maybe even more at home there than in the luxurious five-star Parador Hotel.

The line-up moved slowly up the stairs to the Pilgrim Office. Finally at the desk, I was greeted by a very friendly and cheerful young dark-haired woman who spoke perfect English. She gave me a form to fill in my name, country, age, and reason for walking. She signed the Compostela and noted my name in its Latin variation—Susannah—then handed it back to me. Since high school I'd been going by the name Sue. Strangely though, on the Camino, I had returned to using the Latin form of Susan the name I was given at birth and this completed another circle in my life. As I left the building I was shocked to see Santiago and Alberto there in the line-up outside.

"Hey, guys, what are you doing here so late in the day?" I asked them.

"We got lost on the way," Santiago shook his head and then said, "and it took us ten hours to travel what should have been a four-hour walk." Alberto just shrugged his shoulders and looked to the ground with an embarrassed smirk. Both Alberto and Santiago had been an important part of my journey. Even though Alberto didn't receive the Eagle Feather, I got the sense that in the process he had learned something about himself. I kissed them each goodbye and walked directly to the Cathedral.

Behind the altar, there was another line-up to hug the statue of the Apostle. They were doing repairs on his jewelled silver cape and it looked strange without it. The line-up for the Apostle extended back towards the rows of Confessionals in the Cathedral and each had a sign posting the different languages spoken by the priest on duty. Again, despite the profound rewards, I absolutely refused to participate in a private Confession.

I had unearthed an even older usage of the word confession that was derived from the Latin word, *confessio*. This word was originally used to designate the burial place of a saint. This providential discovery, especially since I was visiting the tomb of Saint James, was confirmation in a way that I'd already been to Confession and I didn't have to admit guilt in the conventional sense.

While standing in line, again I automatically began reciting the Hail Mary prayer, over and over, like it was a mantra. I was nudged by the person in line behind me to move forward to catch up to the people who had moved ahead. Crouching through the low doorway, I walked up the worn marble stairs to the Apostle's chamber and stood momentarily behind the immense statue which had been designed by the Cathedrals architect Master Mateo. Rather awkwardly, I embraced it while thanking all the pilgrims, villagers, family and people at home who had helped me on my journey. There was a line-up behind me waiting for their turn so I quickly blessed myself and turned to leave. "*Miigwech Creator,*" I whispered knowing the Creator was listening.

Downstairs there was another long queue to see the remains of the Apostle, so I decided on my return journey to go to the pilgrim's Mass and pay my respects at that time. On my way out, I paused to bump heads with a statue of Master Mateo. Camino folklore says that if you ask him an important life question, he'll give you the answer. I spoke out loud to be sure he heard me.

"How will I know when I have found the right person for the Eagle Feather?" I said. I waited and waited. There was no answer.

On my journey, I carried a stone for my friend Pat whose funeral I'd attended the day I left Canada. I walked through the Cathedral and ritualistically left her stone on the ledge of a marble pillar near the altar. I said a prayer and asked God to guide her on the next part of her life journey. Exiting through the Porto de la Gloria, I stepped into the bright sunlight and bustling Obradoiro Square. It was as though an entire lifetime had passed while I was inside the Cathedral. I was anxious to start walking again since I still had over three-hundred and fifty kilometres to cover and I hadn't found a recipient for the Eagle Feather. Walking back towards my hostel, I stopped in at the Santiago Tourist Office and asked for information about the pilgrim way to Fisterra.

"We don't have information about the Camino itself," the woman said in perfect English. "This is the Santiago Tourist Office." Her eyes moved to watch someone behind me and she said, "You might want to speak to that woman." A stunningly beautiful Spanish woman with a statuesque build and long dark brown hair pulled back off her face appeared to glide down the stairs behind me. She approached the counter with a warm smile and the woman quickly explained my situation to her in Spanish.

She turned to me and said, "Hello, my name is Maria. I walked to Fisterra last year and would be happy to offer you some personal advice." She suggested I go to an Internet café and search the word Xacobeo. I knew from the Camino list-serves that this was the Gallego word for Santiago, or Saint James. At first, I thought she was sending me away and as if reacting to my expression, she turned to the computer on the counter and began doing the search herself. She printed out a copy of a map.

With great efficiency, she named each of the villages I would pass along the way and provided detailed information as I hurriedly wrote it down. She pointed out the town of Negreira and warned me to be sure to get enough food and water there, since there were no stores for the next thirty-five kilometres after that. She recommended from Cabo Finisterre there was an old branch of the pilgrim's way that I should walk. It was an extraordinary thirty-five kilometre route that ends at the seaside village of Muxia on the Costa da Morte. I assured her that I was planning to go there and she suggested I visit the Sanctuary of Nosa Senora da Barca. I nodded appreciatively and thanked her for her advice.

Listening to her speak, I was reminded that on my life journey, people like Bruce, Sherry, Judith, and now Maria, had appeared like angels sent to guide me along the way.

16

Self-Selecting Destiny

Tucked in my sleeping bag I slept peacefully with the Eagle Feather to protect me. It felt good to be warm. Since there wasn't a window in the glorified closet, I had no idea of the time or what the weather was like outside. Nonetheless, the anticipation of leaving Santiago to trace the footsteps of the past, filled me with excitement and I jumped out of bed.

It was only 6:30 a.m. when I swung the pack over my shoulders and opened the door to leave. I picked up the walking stick that Santiago had given me and just as I was locking the door, the hostel owner appeared. Looking at the rugged stick I had in my hand, he offered me another one that someone had left behind. It was in much better condition and the handle was sanded to a smooth finish to avoid blisters. The deciding factor was that it had a scallop shell engraved into the handle. I left Santiago's stick in the hall hoping it would be given to another needy pilgrim and I left.

The ancient and worn cobblestones on the street were damp and shone in the streetlights. It was still dark and there were very few people on the street so the click of my walking stick on the stone roads echoed off the walls of the ancient buildings. I followed the yellow arrows westbound on Huertas Street, out of the city towards Fisterra. At the city limits, I turned around to look at the view I would be seeing when I walked back this way on the return route. It was also a chance for me to pause and acknowledge where I had already been. The sun hadn't quite risen over the city but it had cast a golden light on the Cathedral. It was a most glorious sight. I took the Eagle Feather out of my pouch and ritualistically honoured it. I spoke to it from a place deep within me.

"*Miigwech Creator*," I said. "I trust you will guide me." After putting it away, I turned around to begin walking filled with eager anticipation and a sense of hope that everything would work out. It was a gorgeous sunlit day and it was warm so I took off my jacket and tied it around my waist. Within minutes, as I fell into the familiar rhythm of walking, my mind eased into a meditative state.

My thoughts drifted back to when I tried out for the Argonaut Rowing Club masters crew that would go the FISA World Masters Rowing Championships in 2001. Our coach, Paul Westbury, made it clear to us from the very beginning of the try-outs that we would self-select to be a part of this crew. By this, he meant that each one of us would ultimately decide for ourselves if we wanted to be in the boat or not. Based on our personal intentions and commitment to training, he said that we, not him, would be the ones to choose. By doing this he gave us the choice and permission to create the future that we earnestly desired. He believed that what we believed in our mind, our body would deliver and each one of us had the power to manifest destiny. I trusted his advice and made it my intention to be a world-class rower. I decided that I wanted to be in the eight women sweep boat and started acting as if it was so. With this intention and the training I did, eventually I was selected, or rather I self-selected, for the crew. We won a gold medal at the world masters championships that year.

With Paul's self-selection theory in mind, I began to consider that maybe the person who was to receive the Eagle Feather might also self-select their destiny. Perhaps my position in this process was to be more like Paul's role as a coach. It wasn't for me to judge who should get the Eagle Feather, but to believe the recipient would make the choice and then open the possibility for them to self-select for this great honour.

After an hour of walking in the hot sun, I was finally outside the city and I saw a sign across the street for a *taberna*. I went in. There was a long wooden bar that gleamed under layers of varnish. A middle-aged man was up on a ladder and had the door to the men's bathroom propped open. He was painting the walls in a dark red color, which struck me as unusual for a bathroom. He carefully climbed down and served me a freshly made *cafe con leche*. I took off my boots and put my feet up on a chair. A few minutes later he returned and offered me a complimentary chocolate croissant. I thanked him and then started speaking in pidgin Spanish.

"*Quando* kilometres to the next village?" I asked. From what I could make out from his response I thought it was twelve kilometres away. I finished my drink and put my boots on. It was now mid-day and it was very dry walking in the hot sun. Up ahead, on the other side of the road, a pilgrim was walking toward me. I assumed she must be walking the reverse route. As we got closer, I called out to her, "*Hola*," I said without even thinking about which language I was speaking. "Where are you coming from?" I blurted out. To my surprise she answered in English with a bit of an accent.

"The end of the world," she said laughing at her own words. I immediately crossed the road eager to meet another pilgrim who could speak English and had been where I was going. Maybe she could offer me some sage advice. When she got closer she introduced herself.

"My name is Janine and I'm from Australia," she said warmly in a thick accent. She too was fair-skinned, had ash blonde hair but she was a little taller than me.

"I'm Sue, from Canada," I replied and we shook hands. Since I was on the lookout for potential recipients for the Eagle Feather and longing for company, I wanted to take every opportunity I could to spend time with the people I met along the way.

"There's a bar about a hundred metres back that way," I said pointing to it. "Do you want to join me for a cafe con leche?

"Sounds perfect," she said. "Let's go."

As we walked, Janine told me the story about how she had been saving her money for years to go on a trip around the world. She started in Japan and was on her way to Africa. She was travelling through Europe and at the last minute, had decided to include walking the Camino as part of her plans. We went inside the bar and I noticed another older man had arrived there since I'd left. When he saw us, he stopped talking to the paint-spattered owner and turned his ample charm on us.

"Oh, what beautiful ladies you are," he exclaimed holding his hands up to his face in exaggerated surprise. We laughed and thanked him for the compliment. Smiling broadly, he insisted on paying for our *cafe con leche* and we accepted. Janine and I immediately sat down at the table and continued our conversation.

She had traveled for over two years and was now hoping to make it to Africa by May. After that, she planned to go back to her home in Australia, unless of course her travels took her somewhere she hadn't planned. She said when she first started walking the French Route of the Camino, a hospitalera offered her a pair of boots that had been left at an albergue by a pilgrim who had some trouble with blisters. They fit her perfectly and she had been using them ever since. Since she'd be walking the reverse route to Santiago and then to Portugal, I gave her my list of pilgrim hostels and the map that Maria had provided. She in turn offered me a list of the villages and towns on the route I would be taking to Fisterra and Muxia with the total kilometres noted.

"What have you discovered about yourself on such a long journey?" I asked with curiosity.

"Crikey!" she replied. "That's some question." Janine went on to say that she'd discovered even though she'd been travelling for two years, she still wasn't at peace with herself. She felt as though she was still looking for something more. She said she was always collecting more things to add to her backpack, which was a big problem because of the weight. I was intrigued by her courage and drawn to this middle-aged woman who was committed to seeing the world on foot and wearing a backpack. I found myself mentally checking off the criteria for the Eagle Feather as she spoke. She was even a storyteller. She told me that was keeping a detailed diary and was considering writing a book one day and I told her about writing *My Camino* and offered to help her in any way I could. Unable to wait any longer, I shared my story about the Eagle Feather with her. She was enthralled with the account the dream and how I had received the message from Sherry.

"How will you decide who gets it?" she asked.

"That's a very good question and one I am still working through," I replied. I told her about my rowing coach's theory of the possibility to self-select destiny, hoping she would react in some way that would give me a clue. Instead Janine made it clear that she didn't want to add more weight to her already heavy load, literally or figuratively. Consciously or maybe unconsciously, she had chosen not to be the recipient of the Eagle Feather. That was enough for me to trust I was doing the right thing based on the notion of self-selection. I only hoped that I had the patience to wait and not force the issue with whomever I met. This would be a test for me.

17

Meeting a Monk

After climbing up a large hill and walking through the entire medieval town to the other side, I finally reached the albergue in Negreira. Tired and hungry, it was a welcome sight to see such a clean bright space provided for the pilgrims. In Galicia, the Xunta or government affiliates never asked for any payment to stay at an albergue, although donations were gratefully accepted. I remembered Maria's words of advice to buy food here, since there wasn't another store for many kilometres. I dropped my backpack on a bunk bed to declare it as my space, and went out to find a market. Climbing down the steep hill put a lot pressure on my knee and before long I was too tired to walk any further. I went into the first bar I came upon, hoping that they carried groceries.

Behind the bar, there was a woman washing the shelves while her young children played nearby. In my poor Spanish, I asked what food she carried but she couldn't understand me. She motioned for me to go behind the bar and pick out what I needed. I did and chose enough to get me through the next day: crackers, bread, chocolate, bananas, yogurt, and juice. I bought a bag of pasta and some tomato sauce would provide for dinner that night.

Back at the albergue I ate the pasta and then went to the common room. I sat down on a sofa and introduced myself to a man who was sitting there reading.

"*Hola,*" I said, not sure what language he spoke. He smiled and leaned toward me.

"Hi, I'm Matthew," he said with a thick Irish accent while shaking my hand. I loved meeting people who connected me with my Celtic heritage. I introduced myself.

His dark eyes sparkled as he raised an inquisitive eyebrow.

"Would you be the writer who has just finished a book on the Camino?" I nodded in reply. He said he had talked to Janine, the Australian pilgrim who'd told him about me. I was curious if she'd mentioned the Eagle Feather too. Matthew went on to say that he was a Benedictine Monk and had just finished his religious studies at the divinity college in England. He was walking the Camino before he returned home to Ireland. Within a few weeks, he would be assigned to a monastery anywhere in the world and might be stationed there for several years. Curious, I asked him how the role of a monk compared to that of a priest. He said that a monk is not a priest and not a layman, but somewhere in between. I didn't know what that meant but hopeful, encouraging thoughts about Matthew as the recipient raced through my mind. Here was a compassionate, spiritual leader who was living his chosen vocation. Plus, in Sherry's dream she was told that the recipient would be from a country that I wasn't from. She also said the person would take the Eagle Feather to another country where they weren't from. It all fit perfectly with Matthew's situation. Right away I thought that he was an ideal recipient for the Eagle Feather. Actually, I was absolutely sure of it. I couldn't help but tell him everything I knew about the Eagle Feather. He was intrigued with my quest, asking a lot of questions about Sherry's dream and its origin. I tried to answer each one clearly, describing what Sherry had seen in her vision. I explained that its home was the red cloth wrap with a deerskin tie around it. Then I informed him that the only stipulation was that the Eagle Feather cannot be exposed to alcohol or mood-altering drugs, and Sherry had been very clear about this criteria.

"Well, there's no way I could be its keeper then," he said shifting uncomfortably in his chair.

"Why not?" I asked.

"I'm Irish and I really like my beer," He replied.

I was shocked with his answer. I couldn't believe that he truly felt this way. The last thing I expected was an outright declaration that he didn't want it. My first reaction was disappointment. Why didn't he want the Eagle Feather? Why was he was resisting this great honour? Convinced his comment was only an excuse, I was sure that I could figure out how to make this work. It would just take some more time. While I recovered from the shock of his rejection and before I could suggest an alternative, Matthew abruptly stood up and said he had to go.

Before leaving on this journey, I had agreed to trust the Creator to present the right person for the Eagle Feather. I was so certain that Matthew was the ideal candidate that I wouldn't give up. I knew he would cross my path again.

18

A Love Affair on the Camino

In the wee hours of the next morning I began to pack quietly, trying not to wake the sleeping pilgrims. The sound of the zippers on my sleeping bag seemed loud, although not as loud as the ubiquitous snoring of the other pilgrims. With thirty-five kilometres to walk that day, I guessed it would take more than eight hours to cover the distance and that didn't include rest breaks.

It was difficult to find my way in the darkness. I got lost leaving Negreira until the glow from the early morning sun barely provided enough light to see the yellow arrows. Stopping by a fence, I took out the Eagle Feather and held it up to the rising sun. I prayed for courage and strength to help me make it through the day.

"Miigwech Creator," I said with a deep breath.

I began walking along the ancient stone path that led into a forest. Before long, I arrived at a spectacular view where an 800-metre waterfall cascaded down the side of the mountain. Captivated by its beauty, I stopped, faced the mighty mountain and stood still in a state of surrender. Centering my body to connect with the ground below my feet, I opened my hara and my heart to embrace all the love of the universe, just as I had done on Cebreiro. Standing there, an explosion of absolute love surged through me again and a tremendous sense of overwhelming joy imbued everything—the sky, the mountains, as well as me. Satiated in mind, body and soul by the magnificence that surrounded me, I smiled in gratitude. I looked down at the ground and saw a small white granite stone. With humble gratitude, I picked it up, rubbed it and began walking with it.

After a tough two kilometre climb up the mountain, I reached the small seemingly deserted town of Zas. It was quiet and lonely. Since I wasn't sure of the actual distance I had left to cover and I didn't need to rest, I walked through the village. The only stop I made was to leave the white stone on the side of the road in the village. The dirt path eventually narrowed to about twenty centimetres in width and I had to carefully balance myself as I moved forward, putting one foot directly in front of the other. Pre-occupied with this simple challenge, time moved slowly and my mind became empty, serene and content. I had no thoughts. With each step I took, I bonded closer to Mother Nature through the connection of my feet on the ground. We became one.

Arriving at the next village, Vilaserio, I stopped at the local bar, found a seat near the window and took off my boots. A peregrina entered. She had a short stylish haircut with a touch of gray showing at the temples that gave her a sophisticated look. She was also limping. I invited her to sit with me at my table and introduced myself.

"I'm Sue, the Canadian," I said proudly.

"I'm Nathalie, from Brittany, France," she replied with a lovely French accent. "Do you know where that is?"

"Yes, I travelled there several years ago with my husband and daughters. We stayed in a Bed and Breakfast close to Mont Saint Michel."

"It's *magnificent, non*?" she said. Thrilled that I knew about this place we immediately launched into a conversation about the famous medieval castle surrounded by the sea at high tide. It was as if we had been friends forever.

"*Excuse moi*, Nathalie," I said standing up to look for the washroom. "*Servicio?*" I called to the owner. He pointed to an old weathered wooden door. It opened into a tiny room with a high ceiling and white tile floor. There was an odd-shaped tiled box on the floor with two raised porcelain pads shaped like footprints on either side of a small hole about the size of a large melon. The toes faced toward me, angled slightly outward. Hesitantly, I put my feet on the footpads, lowered my pants to my knees and squatted down aiming at the hole I could barely see between my legs. It felt good to rest my weight on my bent legs. To my delight and relief, the system was perfectly designed. To top it all off there was toilet paper on the shelf and this was a regarded luxury for a pilgrim like me.

Back at the bar, Nathalie and I packed our things and decided to walk together for a while. While on the path, we walked in the direction of the city of Hospital, although our final destination that day was Olveiroa. Nathalie told me that she had started her Camino walking from St. Jean Pied de Port, France, to Villa Franca, Spain, last year. Because of limited vacation time she had returned this year to complete the last half of the Camino and she was walking all the way to Fisterra. On her travels this time she had met Julian, a Spaniard from Madrid. On the first day they walked together on the Camino, they had fallen madly in love with each other. He had to return home to go back to work and couldn't walk with her to Fisterra. Nathalie talked continuously about her time with Julian and how much she missed being with him. Even though she was lonely without him, she had decided to continue walking to Fisterra as originally planned.

"It is said that everyone has a love affair on the Camino, even if it is with yourself," I told her. Then I shared my story of practising the art of self-love on the first Camino and all the details about my incredible love story with Andreas. For hours we walked and talked shared the intimate stories of our lives. The time went by quickly.

We climbed almost five-hundred metres upwards on Monte Aro, toward a perfectly clear blue sky. Birds and bees flew in front of us, as if guiding the way. Far off, we heard the faint sound of rushing water as we descended into the valley of the river Xalles. It was a peaceful and joyous place to be. While walking, I told Nathalie about the mission I was on to find a recipient for the Eagle Feather.

"Where did it come from?" she asked and then questioned, "Why do the Natives honour the Eagle? How will you know who to give it to?" Her inquisitive nature was quite demanding and at the same time, refreshing. I tried to answer all of her questions. I told her the story about how the Eagle flew the highest of all and it had made an offer to the people to act as a go-between or emissary, carrying messages and desires of the Native people to the Creator's attention.

"That way," she said, "the humans would be assured that they were not alone in the world." Nathalie spoke, grasping at its significance intuitively. I was glad for her company, even if our conversation often returned to more stories about her romantic Camino love. Like me, Nathalie also had a knee injury and blisters so we walked about the same pace. We shared life lessons, dark chocolate and anti-inflammatory medication too.

Walking on a dirt road, we crossed a sixteenth century bridge over the river Xalles and finally arrived in the village of Olveiroa. We followed the signs for the pilgrim's albergue, climbing a steep hill to find several renovated stone structures. The wooden doors and trim on the windows were painted a vivid peacock blue colour and reflected the vibrant folk art of northern Spain, making it easy to identify all the buildings connected to the albergue. Inside the main building there was a bowl of oranges and note handwritten in both English and Spanish, saying that the hospitalera would be back in an hour. After signing the guest book, we stamped our credentials, helped ourselves to an orange and sat down on a bench to rest.

Eventually, we went across the narrow dirt road to another building that looked like it had been a horse stable at one time. We picked out a bunk bed and unpacked our simple belongings. We then proceeded to check out the other buildings. We entered a large room with a long wooden table and benches on either side. Next to it was another, more formal decorated dining room area. The deep-set windowsills displayed charming decorative pieces that included vases, china statues and pilgrim keepsakes. On the kitchen counter, there was a long stick of fresh baked bread on a cutting board. An inviting bowl of fresh farm eggs sat in the middle of the table. We looked in the small fridge and found some vegetables and a large ceramic bowl of thick fatty slices of bacon.

"Would you like me to make an omelette for dinner?" Nathalie excitedly suggested.

"That would be perfect," I responded enthusiastically.

"Please rest," Nathalie pleaded, "and let me serve you." I watched with delight as Nathalie moved around the kitchen with ease. I cut some bread and set the table. Some other pilgrims arrived to prepare their own dinner. First, there was a German couple and then a family from Belgium, travelling with their teen-aged daughter, arrived. We all shared food, laughter and endless pilgrim stories.

19

The End of the World

Celtic legends say Santiago was the place there the dead gathered to follow the Sun to the sea. The ancient pilgrims who walked the French Route often continued westward past the holy city. They'd arrive at the most westerly point of land which they believed was the end of the world—*Cabo Finisterre*. In Gallego it's known as Fisterra and in Latin it's known as *finis terrain*. This time tomorrow, I would arrive there like the pilgrims of old and follow in the footsteps of my own Celtic ancestors. It was almost the half-way point of my entire journey. First, however, I would have to complete a long forty-one kilometre hike crossing over difficult mountainous terrain.

Today my blisters were a mess. I covered them with gel-pads and painfully squeezed my swollen feet into my boots. Nathalie and I had a big breakfast together and then left at 7:30 a.m. in the morning ready to climb the mountains. We crossed the river Logoso and arrived at the fork in the road where we took the way to Fisterra. By noon, we had covered nineteen kilometres climbing up and down the undulating mountain range. The sun was out and it was hot so we had stripped down to the lightest clothes we had. Because of our injuries, we agreed we would walk at our own pace but always with the other person somewhere in sight.

As we descended through the pine groves of Alto do Cruceiro da Armada, we separated. I noticed there was a paved road up ahead. It veered downward on a steep decline that looked like it never ended. Grateful for the distraction, I became focused on getting to the bottom of it. After about ten minutes I arrived at a plateau exhausted, thirsty and desperately needing a rest. I turned around to look for Nathalie, but she wasn't there. Rounding a corner, I spied for the first time the beautiful seaside city of Cee still further below and covered with its white sandy shoreline. I stood there momentarily, stunned by the familiar scent of the ocean and the awe-inspiring beauty of the alabaster beach.

On my right there was a bar so I went inside to wait for Nathalie. I found a seat by the window and dropping my pack on the floor I walked over to the counter and ordered a *cafe sola* before visiting the bathroom. Just as I returned to my seat, the door nosily opened and a woman entered.

"Are you Sue the Canadian?" she asked.

"Yes," I answered, surprised that she knew me.

"I have a message for you," she said and suddenly a rush went through my body. I thought maybe it had something to do with the Eagle Feather. "Your friend Nathalie, has been struggling with her injured knee," she said. I immediately felt bad for leaving her alone. "She's not far behind you and wanted me to ask you to wait for her at this restaurant."

"Of course. Thank you," I said and she left. While waiting for Nathalie, I noticed behind the counter, two women spoke non-stop to each other in Spanish, often cutting each other off. Based on their tone of voice and animated facial expressions, I suspected they were catching up on some steamy local gossip. I took off my boots and although curious to see what the blisters looked like, I didn't dare take off the gel-pads, since I'd never get them back on the same way again. The door of the bar creaked open.

"Bonjour Susannah," a voice called out. I recognized the familiar voice of Nathalie. I jumped up from my seat glad to see her and we

hugged tightly. I helped take off her pack and she dramatically plunked herself onto a chair with a big sigh. "Oh, it was *très difficile. N'est pas?*" she said half in French. "I struggled to make it down the mountain, but knowing you were there ahead of me, gave me the strength to keep going," she sighed, smiling at me. We talked for a long time and when we were finally well-rested, we packed and left. I insisted that Nathalie have my walking stick to help take some pressure off her sore knee. Within minutes of being outside, I saw a stone. I bent over, becoming even more aware of the weight on my back, I picked it up and gave it to her. She started rubbing the stone between her fingers and then put it in her pocket.

We were content to walk more slowly and moved into a philo-sophical conversation. Since Nathalie was going home to France the next day, she was concerned about returning to the ordinary world. She made a personal declaration to go back home and live the sim-ple pilgrim virtues she had learned on the Camino. She felt confi-dent that she was truly a pilgrim in spirit and wanted to live her life that way forever.

Eventually we arrived in Cee. This was the place where the Santi-ago-Fisterra Route joins the Classical Route on the Coast of Death to finally end at the city of Muxia. As we neared the beach, I imme-diately noticed the tangy scent of salty sea air that was carried on a warm breeze from across the water. We dropped our packs in the sand and ran to the water's edge. I didn't want to remove my blister dressings, so I just sat on the beach taking in the scenery and feeling content to be near the water. Nathalie tore off her socks and boots and ran into the water, jumping around with excitement and forget-ting about her knee for the moment. With her thin, petite figure, she looked like a young girl dancing in the waves. The water was very cold so she soon returned to the beach to dry off. Directly behind us, there was a hotel with a store that sold *helato*. I asked Nathalie if she knew what that was.

"It's ice cream, Susannah," she said happily. Since it was warm that day, we each bought a strawberry cone. It was getting late so we decided to keep walking while we ate our ice-cream. As we walked through the town, the path changed to crushed granite pavement laid inside square frames, making it even more uncomfortable. I swore that I could feel the hard surface of the pavement burning right through the soles of my boots into my feet.

We walked and walked and walked. While there was very little conversation, just merely the company of each other was enough. Sometimes she set the pace and I patterned my stride after her lead. At other times, I acted like the stroke person in a crew boat setting the cadence and she followed me. Our timing, regardless of who was leading, matched perfectly. After what seemed like many hours of walking, we were relieved when we eventually arrived in the city of Fisterra. We were led by arrows through the busy city and down through narrow streets toward the sea. Countless times, we both thought we were almost at the albergue and disappointment set in when we turned another corner, only to find out we weren't there yet. Finally, after an extended walk through the entire city, we arrived at a building set right up against the curb of a narrow street near the port. Relieved, we quickened our pace as we approached the albergue only to find out the door was locked. Nathalie noticed a sign that said it would be open at 5:00 p.m. but I was so exhausted I wanted to crash right there on the sidewalk. She suggested we go to the bar across the street and rest.

Usually, I never drink pop. My body was craving sugar so I ordered a Coke and it came in a small old-fashioned glass bottle. I looked around the room and was surprised to see Matthew, the Benedictine Monk, sitting at the bar. I waved to him to come join us. He shook his head and holding his beer up he indicated that he was almost finished. We finished our drinks and when I looked around for Matthew again, he had left. Nathalie and I made our way back to find the door of the albergue was still locked. A half-dozen other pilgrims sat waiting on the curb, so we found a spot and joined them. Nathalie watched my backpack while I went to the phone booth to call my daughters. I was thrilled to find Simone and Meghan were both home and I talked to each of them separately. It seemed like a very short conversation and after I hung up, I missed them even more. Tara wasn't home so I left her a long voice message. I returned to sit with Nathalie. Cars drove by just barely missing our feet hanging over the curb, but we were too tired to move away.

Finally, at 5:00 p.m. sharp the hospitalera opened the door and a new line-up formed outside her small office. When I stepped inside, she promptly asked me the usual questions: name, country, age, where I started walking and if I was *sola*. I showed her my pilgrim passport and then she signed and presented me with a beautiful certificate—a Finnesterna—which I hadn't known anything about. It's a certificate of completion that is only given to pilgrims who've completed the walk from Santiago to Fisterra. With my certificate in hand, I moved into the compactly furnished common room with everyone else until all the registrations were complete.

As a group we were taken upstairs to where the dorms where. I selected a lower bunk, as usual, next to a window. Immediately I unpacked and staggered into the shower, so weak I could hardly stand. I leaned my head against the wall letting the water massage my aching body. After drying off with the high absorbency towel, I got dressed in my previously worn clothes. When I returned to my bunk I found out that everyone was getting ready to walk to the Cape—the end of the world. They had planned to arrive just as the sun was setting and partake in the ancient pilgrim ritual of burning their clothes. Nathalie wanted to participate but I still needed my clothes to get me back to Portugal.

"Please come with me Susannah," Nathalie begged. "It's only three kilometres more," she said. That really meant it was a total of six kilometres we would have to walk in both directions. I thought about not going but I knew I'd regret it later. Agreeing to join her, I changed into thinner socks and put on my rain-jacket. With about an hour until sunset, we left the city and followed the scallop shell signs the entire way. It was a gradual upward climb. A few cars drove by, honking their horns for encouragement. The wind was strong and as the sun set the air grew colder. Many times I wanted to stop, but Nathalie continued to walk and I resolutely followed. If she hadn't been there, I would have given up.

Finally, up ahead I could see the rocky point where a lighthouse stood. We were now at the terrestrial boundary of the European continent and it was truly exciting. We climbed the smooth rocks and found a place to sit on the top of the cliff facing westward. Looking out and watching the shadowy water crash wildly against the jagged coast, I could completely understand why in medieval times the Atlantic Ocean was referred to as the Dark Sea.

The blisters on my feet were severely aggravated. We had walked thirty-five kilometres that day already and walking to the Cape meant we had walked almost the equivalent of a marathon. My body was breaking down. I took off my shoes and socks to air my feet. A few others pilgrims trickled over. The conversation was hushed as we all anticipated the defining sunset moment. The sky was dark blue and the few clouds moved with the force of the strong wind. Nathalie struggled to get a fire started. When she finally did, I watched in silence as she burned her clothes. It was an important ritual for Nathalie but it was strange for me to watch her set fire to the clothes that had kept her warm on this journey.

Sitting there on the rocky cliff, the wind blew all around me. At this point in my journey, I had developed a strong spiritual connection to the Creator and decided to carry out my own ritual. Still wrapped in its red cloth home, I held the Eagle Feather in front of me, clutching it tightly with two hands so it wouldn't blow away. I made a promise to the Creator that I would continue to carry the Eagle Feather on its journey, for however long it would take to find the recipient. Quietly, I thanked the Creator for believing in me. Then I said a prayer of gratitude for the blessings in my life; my children, my family, my friends, Sherry, and for sending Bruce to help me to manifest my Camino voice. Finally, I prayed to the Creator for the wisdom and guidance to complete this quest. I carefully tucked it into the pouch around my waist. Ritualistically, I picked up a stone, rubbed my sorrow into it and threw it into the crashing waves far below.

20

Coast of Death

It was going to be a long day with another thirty-five kilometre walk to Muxia ahead of us. Thankfully the weather was co-operating and it was a gorgeous sunny day. I didn't care whether I was walking alone or not anymore. There wasn't the same need for me to have a solo journey. By now, I was becoming more anxious about finding someone for the Eagle Feather and I needed to be around people. Almost at the half-way point of my journey, I was afraid that I had failed and that I would let Sherry and the Creator down. Doubt about my ability to complete this mission still troubled me everyday and it was becoming a burden. Once again I remembered the wise words of my rowing coach Paul. After he informed me that I would be in the boat that was going to the world's, I felt beholden to him.

"Don't worry Paul," I assured him. "I won't let you down,"

To my surprise he replied, "Sue, don't do this for me. Do it for yourself." Paul had said that we would self-select our place in the boat and now he was suggesting I should also race for myself. Again his words reassured me that I must first respect and honour myself, even though I was committed to the crew. I couldn't complete my mission by thinking about what anyone else thought about who should get the Eagle Feather. This quest was a part of my personal journey and I had to do this for myself first. I knew if I did this from a place of love, then I could trust that everything else would fall into place.

The discipline of not judging others as potential recipients was much more difficult than I'd imagined. I thought that I wasn't judging, but again and again, this virtue was being tested on this quest and I wasn't passing. The theory of self-selection, in principle, was much easier than having to actually apply it in real life. It seemed no matter what happened in the past, I still had to practice the discipline of being a simple pilgrim, by acting without judgment of others or myself and living from a place of love. It wasn't any easier the second time on the Camino.

This quest wasn't just about trying to decide how to find the recipient for the Eagle Feather, the entire journey was becoming more a life lesson for me. I was beginning to really believe the recipient had already been chosen and maybe the purpose of the dream message was to help direct them to the Eagle Feather. If that was so, all I had to do was trust that the Creator would guide them to me. Why was that so difficult?

Natalie and I reached the top of a hill just as the morning sun was about to crest over the horizon. We stopped to admire the dawn of a new day. I asked Nathalie to wait while I took out the Eagle Feather and performed my morning ritual. I started by thanking the Creator for trusting me with the Eagle Feather. Holding it close to me, with all of my love, I kissed it.

"*Miigwech Creator,*" I said, repeating the familiar Ojibway words.

"Would it be possible to hold the feather before you put it away?" Nathalie asked. I gave it to her gently placing it in the palms of her hands. Up until now I hadn't really considered the possibility that Nathalie could be a recipient.

"Be careful, it's very delicate," I warned her.

"It's very light," she said, gently turning it over. I watched her handling it. With a loving delicate touch, she smoothed the ruffled edges of the vanes and held it to close her. When she handed it back, I kissed it again and carefully wrapped it in the red cloth. She said nothing about wanting or not wanting it and I resisted the urge to ask her.

Nathalie had decided that she'd walk one more day up the coast with me and then she would take the bus to Santiago tomorrow to make it back in time for work on Monday. We walked along the coastal roads and into a forest again. I was glad not to be alone on the path. We got lost at one point but soon we came upon a concrete post decorated with a cracked blue ceramic tile with the scallop shell symbol. Below that, a yellow arrow pointed north next to the word Muxia. Another arrow pointed south with the word Fisterra beside it. Nathalie wanted a picture so she set the timer on her camera and we posed in front of the sign. Just as the camera clicked, I heard a familiar voice calling out to us. It was Matthew, the Benedictine Monk crossing my path once again. He was in a great mood, in contrast to his strange behaviour back in the bar. For the first time, I realized he wore rimless glasses. That day he had on a light pink cotton shirt and khaki shorts. He waved and then walked right past us.

"Matthew," I called out to him, still trying to be open. "Please come back. We want to get a picture of you."

"No, thanks just the same," he said quickly in his lilting Irish accent, "I'm not one for having my picture taken."

"Oh, Matthew," Nathalie called tilting her head coyly. "We really would like to have a picture of you. It will take *un moment. Sil vous plait,*" she begged.

He reluctantly came back, likely out of embarrassment at our persistence. I tried to think of a way to bring up the subject of the Eagle Feather again. It seemed the more pressure I put on judging him as the recipient, the more he resisted. I was still trying to select the person. It occurred to me that maybe this was a lesson for me. For some reason Matthew was self-selecting to decline the honour of the Eagle Feather and I had no choice but to accept it.

At first when Sherry gave me the package with the Eagle Feather, I questioned if I was worth this great honour. When she told me I was being sent on my journey to give it away to someone else, I was somewhat relieved, thinking it would be easy to find another more worthy recipient. I assumed that everyone I met would want it. Strangely, I was beginning to see something different. I found that pilgrims were fascinated by the story of how it came into my possession and its significance to the First Nation people, but no one wanted it. It appeared the honour of caring for it was feared more than it was desired. I began to wonder if it was bearing the responsibility for the Eagle Feather that people feared most. Was it the fear of being honoured? Was it the fear of being a leader? Was it the fear of being accountable for it? I really didn't know the answer.

The sky was light blue and clear all morning, but in the afternoon heavy dark clouds rolled in. We all walked together for a while. Matthew's pace quickened and he was soon out of sight. I stumbled along consumed by the inspiring thoughts about the possibilities for my life that ran through my mind. Nathalie walked ahead of me and following her steps I began a walking meditation, a familiar discipline for me. My mind was still. There were no thoughts at all and I knew this was a time of creativity. I opened my heart. I hadn't been sleeping well so the chance to meditate, even as I walked, allowed me to rest and ultimately gave me more energy.

The benefits of meditative breathing weren't new to me. I'd learned how to do it during even the most physically taxing activities. During labour with my middle daughter, Meghan, my cervix was dilating too slowly, so I had to be induced. The contractions suddenly came on very hard and fast. I'd studied the Lamaze method of natural childbirth where we were taught to use a point of focus and specific breathing techniques to get through the pain of the contractions. During labour, I mastered the breathing techniques I had been taught. When the contraction was over, I'd collapse with exhaustion and actually fall asleep to conserve precious energy until the next one came. The doctors and nurses were so impressed by this phenomenon that they brought in a group of medical students to observe me. After three hours of labour I delivered Meghan, a healthy baby girl. I used the same breathing principles to get me through the constant pain from my blisters and knee injury on the Camino and it worked.

Walking everyday was physically as well as emotionally cleansing. The toxins in my system were filtered out of my body. My nose ran all the time and I perspired a lot in the heat. My heart rate slowed down to a calm beat and I fell into the natural rhythm of walking. My body felt completely alive and I was content to be on the path all day long. Some days I thought I could walk forever.

Up ahead, I spotted a slender man with dark hair and caught up with him.

"Hi," I said, forgetting for a moment that everyone spoke Spanish.

"I'm Carlos, from Barcelona," he said in English with an obvious accent. He wore glasses, had a black beard and thick black curly hair. There was an exceptionally large wooden cross hanging from his neck over a white T-shirt.

"Susannah, from Canada," I replied shaking his hand. I found myself staring at the rather imposing crucifix and reminded myself not to judge. He asked where I was going and I told him of my plan to walk to Muxia and then back to Portugal where I'd started. Carlos had journeyed on the Camino from Madrid to Fisterra and now he was walking to Muxia too. My mind was pre-occupied still thinking about possibilities for the Eagle Feather. After talking for a few minutes, I told Carlos I wanted to walk more slowly and added that I hoped we meet on the path again. He went ahead.

Hours passed and I hadn't seen Matthew. I knew this was a sign for me to let go of control. I stopped to rest in a bus stop shelter located on the outskirts of a village in the middle of nowhere. Nathalie showed up and joined me. I unpacked some bread and a tangerine to share with her.

"Let's make a sandwich," Nathalie suggested.

"I don't have any cheese or meat left. What else can we put in it?" I asked.

"*Chocolate!*" she replied with a big smile. Taking the stick of bread out of my hand, she ripped off a piece and shoved a chunk of dark chocolate into the middle. Then she handed it to me and proceeded to make another one for herself. How very decadent, I thought.

"*Voila*, a chocolate sandwich." She said with excitement and then we laughed together. Another pilgrim came by as we were eating and introduced himself as Ricardo. We offered him a chocolate sandwich which he laughingly declined. Instead, he offered us a chocolate coated digestive cookie and then took a picture of the two of us stuffing our faces. He sat down for a rest and told us he was a high school teacher from Madrid. This was his third Camino. He'd walked the Primativo Route, the oldest Camino route from Oveido, on the north coast of Spain.

We packed up again and started to walk but Ricardo decided to continue along the coastal path, while we opted for the one that was more clearly marked. We agreed to meet again in Muxia and said goodbye to him. Nathalie and I started walking together again. The pain from my blisters became very intense and my pace slowed down. Nathalie walked ahead and soon she was out of sight. Trying not to be discouraged, I questioned whether the pain was there to keep me alert or if I had a hand in creating it as a distraction to avoid thinking about failing to find someone for the Eagle Feather. Because of the long days of walking, I was nearing the point of exhaustion and somehow I now detested my beloved Camino. I'd had enough. I just wanted to go home to the comfort of my family and friends. I missed Bruce and wanted to be together with him. Tired of sleeping in strange places in gray metal bunk beds with people snoring all around me, I started to sob. A few tears rolled gently down my cheeks. As my frustration rose, more tears fell and I began stomping my feet as I walked. I bawled out loud, coughing and gasping for air. The more I thought about going home, the more I wept. The more I wept, the more I wanted to be at home. It was an endless cycle.

"Susannah," Nathalie called from up ahead, "I can see the ocean." Grateful for the distraction, I wiped my tears and hurried to catch up. Nathalie adored the sea and had a child-like attitude to being in nature. "Come, see. *C'est très magnifique.*" We had finally reached Muxia and I felt a renewed sense of hope. As a Pisces woman, the ocean was home and it was a therapeutic place for me. I was attracted to water of any kind and here, on the Camino, I was especially drawn to the power of the ocean crashing onto the shore of this ancient path.

"Can you see the beach way over there?" Nathalie asked pointing with excitement. We still had at least a kilometre to walk to get to the ocean but I could see it clearly. The water would be very cold at this time of the year, but I couldn't wait to immerse my feet in its healing properties. Nathalie rushed ahead to catch up with Ricardo who had already arrived at the beach. By the time I got there, they'd taken off their socks and boots and were wading in the water. Nathalie splashed in the waves while loudly singing a French folk song.

I dropped my backpack and sat down on the sand, quickly removing my boots and socks. I peeled off the sticky gel-pad and bandages exposing the open blisters. Standing up, I walked on the outside edges of the soles of my feet to the beach and stepped into the frigid water. My feet instantly went numb. The sting of the salt water seeping into open sores was a welcome form of pain, however, the sand was abrasive and rough on my bare feet. I stood motionless, looking west toward my home across the restless, endless sea. Then I put my hand on the Eagle Feather beneath my clothes and a feeling of absolute love washed over me.

"*Miigwech Creator,*" I said just as the sun broke through from behind a cloud to warm my face. I looked up to the sky and a sense of absolute peace filled me. The crashing water washed around me, pushing, pulling and naturally cleansing my body, mind and soul.

The ebb and flow of the waves tugged and pulled at my feet, sucking them down into the sandy layers of the ocean floor, trapping them in place. It felt like the sea had complete control over me. Without any warning, an excruciating pain shot through my right foot. I immediately assumed I had been stung by a jellyfish and yanked my right foot from the grip of the sand. Exposed to the cool air there was another even more excruciating needle of pain that shot through my foot.

Grabbing onto my big toe with my right hand, I pulled my foot up to the side and looked closer. A shiny, oval-shaped form was stuck to the side of my heel. It was dark, about four centimetres long and it ballooned out the side. I didn't have my glasses so I couldn't see clearly what it was. My whole body was trembling in fear. Frantically, I hopped on one foot out of the water.

"Nathalie, Ricardo. Please, come and help me," I yelled. I sat on the cold sandy beach and twisted my foot around to see what had happened. I touched it and found out it was hard as stone. On closer examination, I realized the thing on the side of my foot wasn't a jellyfish at all. It was a large blister that had developed yesterday. I'd done some blister surgery at the albergue, poking a hole in it with a sewing needle, to drain the fluid. I was shocked to find that sand had worked its way through the tiny pin-hole. The finely granulated stones were trapped under the multiple layers of skin.

"It's gross," I said to my two friends hovering over me. "My blisters are full of sand. How is that possible?" I asked. Having never seen or heard of anything like this before, I didn't know what to do. By now the pain was unbearable and the sting of the salt under the skin was excruciating. How I could possibly walk with stones in my feet for the next nine days? I asked Ricardo how far it was to the next albergue and that's when he informed us there wasn't a hostel for pilgrims in Muxia. He had been told that we could sleep in the local high school gymnasium, on the floor. Nathalie offered to help me walk there.

Hopping on one foot, I made my way back from the beach to where I had left my pack. Nathalie helped me with my socks but there was no way I could put on my boots. Instead, I slid my feet into my spare shoes, a pair of hand-made moccasins. Nathalie helped me hobble up the steep hill and back to the road. The added weight of my backpack made my feet throb with pain. Each step I took felt like sandpaper was scraping the raw flesh inside my blisters so I walked very slowly. We got to the top of the hill but there wasn't a school in sight. I suspected I needed to see a doctor to have the sand surgically removed, but this was a small coastal port and I wasn't sure I'd find one available. A nearby house had a sign posted saying there were rooms for rent. I thought about stopping there so I wouldn't have to walk anymore but Nathalie encouraged me to continue.

Eventually, we found the school and went into the gym where the soccer coach was setting up for an indoor game that night. He showed us a space under the bleachers where we could sleep. Above us, a small crowd cheered and stamped their feet while watching the local team practice. The coach said the game would end around 10:00 p.m. and then pointed to some blue gym mats leaning against the wall, suggesting we prepare our beds anytime we wanted. All he asked was that we lock the front door when we left in the morning. I was impressed at how trusting the people were of pilgrims.

We stored our backpacks behind the mats and went outside to have dinner. Ricardo suggested a restaurant with a varied selection of Galician seafood and we went there. It was easier for me to walk without the weight of my backpack. He told us he had met another pilgrim earlier that day and had invited him to join us for dinner. The evening was a special celebration since Ricardo and Nathalie had officially finished their pilgrimage. Tomorrow they would take the bus back to Santiago and return to their normal lives at home.

While Ricardo was translating the menu for me, the other pilgrim arrived and coincidentally, it was Carlos, the man with the crucifix whom I'd met earlier on the path. He hugged each of us, and then sat down beside me. We talked about how few pilgrims there were on this route. He told me that Matthew, the Benedictine Monk also arrived this evening. My sense of anticipation and expectation involuntarily rose. He said he was staying in a room at the house on the way into town. It was same the place I had considered staying at near the beach. I asked if he was joining us for dinner but Carlos said he preferred to be alone. I didn't ask anymore questions. I had finally accepted that Matthew had self-selected not to receive the Eagle Feather.

21

In the Eye of God

The wind howled through cracks in the window frames and rain-drops drummed on the metal roof. There was something very soothing about this tiny village. The rustle of plastic bags woke me up. Nathalie and Ricardo were preparing to catch the bus to Santiago. Carlos was still asleep. I seriously considered getting on the bus with them to go to the hospital in Santiago. If my journey ended now, it would mean that I'd have to take the Eagle Feather back home, a sign I had failed in my quest. I laid there, eyes closed, with my sleeping bag pulled up over my head, trying to avoid making a decision. Someone poked me through the sleeping bag.

"I'm leaving now," Nathalie whispered in her lovely French accent. I quickly slipped out of my sleeping bag and gave her a big pilgrim hug. We kissed on each cheek and agreed to stay in touch by e-mail. Ricardo said good-bye and offered me a gift; a package of my favourite chocolate covered digestive cookies. I watched as they walked to the other end of the building, listening to the echo of their footsteps bouncing off the walls of the large gym. The front doors creaked open, then closed with a loud clang. I was alone again.

It was still dark. I walked to the girls change room, where I found a bucket and filled it with water and added some sea salt. I sat on the bench soaking my feet thinking about my Dad. He had had compli-cations associated with his diabetes and the lower part of his leg had to be amputated. The horror of visiting him in the hospital, right after the operation, is still a vivid memory. I was afraid my foot would become infected and something horrible like that would happen to me. Sitting there just thinking about the future possibilites, started to drive me crazy. After I dried my feet I went back to the sleeping area under the bleachers. My clean, folded laundry was piled at the foot of my sleeping bag. I gathered my things together quietly, trying not to disturb Carlos who was still asleep. He stirred anyway.

"Are you leaving?" he asked in a sleepy voice.

"Yes, I really need to find a doctor," I told him. Then I remembered he had done my laundry for me. "By the way, thank you for taking my clothes out of the dryer and folding for me them last night."

"How are your blisters? he questioned.

"I'm not really sure."

"Can I have a look at your foot?" he asked with concern. I sat down on the floor beside him. Gently, he took my foot in one hand and lightly touched the blisters with his fingertip, studying them carefully.

"They look fine," he said. "The sea water has probably kept the stones clean and this has helped to heal the blisters from the inside." Carlos said he was confident that if I could put pressure on my foot, then I could walk back to Santiago. Even so, he suggested we go to the Pilgrim Office and ask for their advice about seeing a doctor.

In silence, we both prepared for the day ahead, following a routine that had become automatic by now. After putting the blue mats back and checking to be sure we hadn't left anything behind, we slipped our packs over our shoulders and stepped outside into the drizzling rain. Carlos was the one who remembered to lock the door. It was cold, windy and wet. A gray mist hung over the village and the fishy smell of the sea stung my nostrils. We walked to the

Pilgrim Office and found the door locked. A sign said the office would open at 9:00 a.m. and that was in another hour.

"What do you want to do? Carlos asked.

"I don't know anymore," I sighed. I didn't want to be alone right then and I was having a lot of difficulty making a decision about what to do. "I need a little more time to decide. Would you join me for a coffee?" Carlos gladly accepted and suggested a café just down the road.

Inside, there were a few small square wooden tables with four chairs set neatly around them. On the wall was a mural of an ancient map of Muxia. We went to the back of the restaurant and I hung my wet jacket over a chair near a heater while Carlos ordered *cafe con leche* for us.

Conversation was easy with Carlos. I enjoyed listening to his gentle, soothing voice. He told me he had been walking for several weeks. He purposely left Barcelona without any money on him in order to experience both humility and the kindness of others. He said that he had faith that God would provide. He was on a mission to serve and be served. Then he talked about how his experience had been so far.

"When I was hungry, people gave me food. When I needed a place to sleep, I found shelter. Sometimes, when I just needed someone to talk to or to share some advice, that person was always there," he said. He had experienced something first hand that most people don't get a chance to do. "Now I'm thinking about joining a monastery when I get back home," he added. I was impressed with his commitment. It was interesting for me that this was my second connection with a monk on the Camino.

Our *cafe con leche* arrived and I shared the story of the Eagle Feather and Sherry's dream. I told Carlos that I thought Matthew was the perfect recipient because he was a pilgrim and a leader who had clarity about his vocation in life. As well, I was confident that he would carry the stories of the Native people to other countries. He asked me why I didn't give him the Eagle Feather.

"He didn't seem to want anything to do with it," I said somewhat sadly. I told Carlos how I'd met Matthew a few days ago and that initially he was very interested in learning about the Eagle Feather. "Since that first encounter, however, anytime I'd tried to have a conversation with him about it, he had avoided me." Looking directly at me again, Carlos spoke. Choosing his words very carefully, he said that he believed Matthew was staying away from me on purpose.

"Maybe in your efforts to align Matthew with the Eagle Feather, you tempted him in many ways; physically, spiritually, emotionally, theologically and philosophically. Now he wants to be left alone." Carlos paused. He said that as far as Matthew was concerned, I was like the Devil enticing him to forsake his religious vocation. There was nothing more to say about it. Devil or no Devil, it was abundantly clear to me that I had consistently ignored Matthew's decision to self-select not to be the recipient of the Eagle Feather. This was an important lesson for me to let go of control and trust. We finished our coffee and it was time for me to leave. I pulled out the black velvet bag filled with stones that I'd brought from home. I offered one to Carlos. He took great care making a choice and then he produced a small black leather bag out of his hip pouch and emptied it, spilling stones all over the table.

"Please choose one," he said, tipping his open hands down toward the table. Knowing that the Natives believed that we don't pick the stones, I waited for the right stone to pick me. It was a small round white one. While I rolled it in my hand, Carlos talked about his beliefs and the magical power of believing in stones. I shared the story of the Sorrow Stones with him. I then took out a copy of my storytelling CD I had been carrying and offered it to him as a gift. He was intrigued by the name, *Stone by Stone*. I explained that the cover was a painting done by an Irish woman named Audrey Smith who was a talented and very dear friend of mine.

By telling Carlos about the painting, I began to understand more clearly how I had integrated the profound lessons of this life-altering journey into my life at home. Anytime I was invited to tell stories about the Camino, I had introduced myself by saying, "My name is Sue Kenney and I am a pilgrim." Through my earnest desire to be a pilgrim every day of my life, both on and off the Camino, together with the action of living the pilgrim virtues I had embraced, I had become the woman in the painting.

"Audrey nick-named the woman in the painting Camino Girl and to represent the virtues of a pilgrim she painted her carrying a feather, a wooden walking stick, a white rose and a scallop shell," I said. Carlos studied the cover, admiring her work. "When I first walked to Santiago, I didn't have a wooden stick or a scallop shell. I had taken high-tech trekking poles. This time I left them at home and I was given this wooden staff by a hospitalero in Santiago." I said showing him my staff with the scallop shell carved on the handle. "Camino Girl is carrying a wooden staff with a scallop shell tied to it." He was struck by the coincidence and I continued pointing out the other remarkable similarities.

"See, she also is holding a white rose in her hand, a symbol of pure love." Taking the Rose of Oklahoma stone out of my pouch I showed it to Carlos. "When I was in Santiago, I met a woman named Judith who'd walked the twice before and she gave me this stone as a gift." Carlos looked closely at the rose-shaped stone. "That's not all," I continued. "Audrey included a feather in the painting because she said it symbolized wisdom. She had no idea I would have the honour of actually carrying a Native Eagle Feather on the Camino."

Carlos excitedly rummaged through his hip pouch and pulled out a small white scallop shell. He said that since I'd been to the end of the world like the pilgrims of old, he wanted me to have a scallop shell to complete the painting. Reaching across the table, he placed it in my open hands.

"Thank you Carlos," I said nodding my head to him.

"Arriving in Muxia, you have walked to the very end of the Camino," he reminded me. "Once you begin the journey back home you will complete the final section of the triangle."

"What triangle?" I asked inquisitively.

"The two points are Fisterra and Muxia." He took a pen from his pouch and drew a triangle on a napkin. "The third point of the triangle is Santiago," he said and then began speaking more slowly. "When you are walking the route you are on now, you are in the triangle. This is also known as the Eye of God."

"Are you saying that I'm walking in the Eye of God right now?" I asked, repeating his words to me. He shook his head up and down. Suddenly something shifted in me. This was my chance to be in front of God and the Creator at the same time. "If I'm in the Eye of God, then I can't very well take a bus, now can I?" I said smiling. I was convinced that I had self-selected this journey and I was more certain than ever, that even as I walked in the Eye of God, I had to complete this quest for myself. Having stones in my feet was just a minor setback that now seemed insignificant.

We packed up our things and left the café. Carlos encouraged me to take the time to walk to the coast to see the Sanctuary of Nosa Senora da Barca, dedicated to the Virgin of the Boat. Although I was worried about adding more kilometres to my day, I decided to go with him. We walked through the village market and got closer to the crashing noise of the sea. Although it was misty and cloudy, I could see the outline of the beautiful church built on the edge of the rock almost sitting out in the sea itself. The story told says that when Saint James was preaching Christianity here, the Virgin Mary appeared in a stone boat that was tied to the port. Some say this is where one of the most profound miracles on the Camino took place.

As we got closer, I could feel a powerful energy from the sea filling every cell of my body. I walked to the edge of the stone platform that was suspended over the rocky cliff looking out to sea. As I stood there I couldn't move or speak. It was a special moment. I went over to the wrought-iron gate in front of the main doors and looked inside. I was speechless and felt a deep sense of compassion for the people in this village. I began to pray for those who had lost their lives to the sea. I prayed for the animals and birds that had lost their homes because of the horrible oil spill disaster that happened on this coast over a year ago. It was eerie to think that because of this, the water on the Costa da Morte and physically turned black. Standing on the stone steps in the vestibule, protected from the rain and mist, I felt grateful.

A woman came up to the vestibule and stood behind me. I moved out of the way to give her space to be alone. She knelt down on the stone and began to pray. I wondered if she was praying for someone she had lost to the sea. I stood there and thought about why the next leg of my journey was interrupted in this way. I was forced to be still to face my fear. I listened and tried to be open. I knew I was afraid of walking alone in the reverse direction without the yellow arrows guiding the way. I was really afraid of being alone and becoming lost. Inside I knew that my deepest fear was the same as it was the first time I walked the Camino. I was afraid of facing the truth about myself and the responsibility of using the gifts I have been given, to live my life purpose.

We left the church and walked up the hill and through the town. Carlos suggested the route towards Dunbria, through the forest, and I trusted his advice. I still had thirty-eight kilometres to walk and it was now getting late. I knew I would be walking slower than normal because of the stones in my feet. I didn't want to rush in any way, but I was conscious of the time of day. Usually, I walked four to five kilometres an hour and I could possibly get there in eight hours if I didn't get lost. Carlos showed me a shortcut he had found. After climbing uphill, we arrived at a cement pylon with a scallop shell symbol on it. When we finally stopped, I realized how hot and sweaty I had become. It had been raining lightly while we climbed and suddenly, it stopped. We rested there to catch our breath and admire the view. Carlos turned and stared at me, his dark brown eyes looking confused.

"Susannah, a feeling of immense love has filled me." I could see he was deeply moved.

"Carlos, you are on a mission from God, to serve and be served. As pilgrims we have walked the path together and you have guided me back onto my path. I am forever grateful to you for showing me the Eye of God." I took his hands in mine. "But now, we must both go and find our own way." He nodded in agreement. We said good-bye and he turned away walking quickly down the mountainside. For a moment, I thought about calling him back to give him the Eagle Feather. I'm not sure why, but I hesitated. As if he knew my thought, he stopped, looked back and waved to me for the last time. Through the mist, I watched him leave.

On the Camino, Carlos had his mission with God and I had my mission with the Creator. After this encounter, I was becoming even more convinced that the two were one and the same. With complete acceptance, that day I had finally resigned myself to the fact that the Eagle Feather might come home with me after all. In a state of gratitude, I looked up to the sky and gave thanks to the Creator for the great lessons that had been bestowed on me through the people I met on my journey. With my hand resting on the Eagle

Feather, I spoke out loud repeating the familiar Ojibway words I had said many times before.

"*Miigwech Creator.*"

22

A Fork in the Road

On the way to Olveiroa, I came to a fork in the road. I looked both ways and realized that I couldn't see the yellows arrows anymore since they were placed for the pilgrims coming from the other direction. It was a confusing situation and reminded me of being in the bow seat of a rowing scull facing the stern where I could see what was behind, not ahead. In a crew boat I learned to trust the coxswain who steered the boat and kept us on the right track. It was strange but appropriate, I was doing something in my life backwards again.

Taking a chance, I made an arbitrary decision to select the fork to the left. As I walked, I occasionally turned around to look for the yellow arrows since I wasn't sure where I was going. I tried to pay attention to my surroundings just in case I had to retrace my steps. Twenty minutes passed and I hadn't seen another arrow on the path. I knew I was lost. Instead of stopping, I walked further into the forest until I finally decided it was time to turn around and retrace my steps back to where I'd started. Forty-five minutes later, I was at the same fork in the road. Frustrated, I sat down on the forest floor and started to cry. After a while there was no point in crying anymore so I got up. Self-pity wasn't helping the situation and besides, I was just getting soggy.

This time I went down the road to the right. It began to lightly rain and hours went by without seeing a soul. I was lonely and remained in constant fear of getting lost. It was almost 5:00 p.m. and the sun was just beginning to set. Luckily, I arrived in a village and spoke to someone passing by.

"*Hola. Donde este Ol-ve-ir-oa in kilometres?*" I said, trying to ask how far it was to Olveiroa but had so much trouble saying the town name that they couldn't understand me. Thankfully I saw a sign on the side of the road that said it was eight kilometres to Olveiroa. I was relieved since I'd already walked almost thirty-two kilometres that day. Walking more slowly, several hours passed before I finally I arrived at the albergue. The door was unlocked so I let myself in. A few pilgrims greeted me as I walked through the common room. After a warm shower and a simple meal of Manchego cheese and crusty bread, I soaked my feet and went to bed early. I laid there thinking about another long journey ahead. Tomorrow, I had to get to Negreira, which was at least thirty-five kilometres away. After that it would only be twenty-four kilometres to Santiago. I was looking forward to being back there once again, although this time, I wouldn't be having dinner at the opulent Parador Hostal de los Reyes Catolicos with either Andreas or Judith. I would be alone.

The next morning I got up early and left. Once outside, I took the Eagle Feather from its red cloth home and held it towards the rising sun, praying to the Creator to guide me on my quest. I took a moment to reflect on our journey together. Sherry had said that while I was in possession of the Eagle Feather, I was in direct connection to the Creator. It was such a great honour. I was truly humbled in its presence.

"*Miigwech Creator,*" I called out in gratitude. Looking down at it I caressed it with my fingers, smoothed out the vanes, and lovingly wrapped it in its home. It felt familiar now. I tucked it safely away and began walking. Soon I arrived at a quaint village nestled in a valley. There were no people on the streets and it was very quiet. I approached an intersection where an older man appeared and stood on the sidewalk watching me. I walked over and greeted him.

"*Hola. Donde esta el bar pour cafe con leche?* He grinned with a crooked-toothed smile and pointed in the direction of a barn. I looked where he was pointing since I was convinced he hadn't understood that I wanted a coffee, not a cow. Just then, a tall woman stepped gracefully out the barn door. She held a battered pitch fork and her large hands spoke of years of hard labour. When I asked her where I could find a restaurant she smiled and motioned for me to wait. I stood there watching as she herded the cows into the barn.

When they were locked away, she led me through the tiny village. Along the way I tried to talk but there wasn't much I could say in Spanish and her English seemed negligible. We came to a house which I realized was her home. Entering her kitchen, she motioned for me to sit at the wooden table. She took a pitcher from the fridge, poured some milk into a pot on the stove and then added coffee in a stove-top espresso maker. When the coffee was brewed and the milk was heated, she poured the steaming coffee into a small bowl. Slowly and deliberately she added the hot milk. She put out some sugar and passed the bowl to me. Then she sat down at the table and waited. I cupped my hands around the warm china and inhaled the comforting, pungent aroma.

"*Ahhh ... Gracias,*" I sighed letting go of my breath. Realizing I hadn't introduced myself I said, "Me Susannah," pointing to myself. Then I looked to her as if to ask her name.

"Anna," she responded as though singing the word. She looked at my blonde hair and blue eyes and asked. "*Allemande?*" I shook my head.

"No not Germany, Canada," I announced with pride and she grinned. I looked around the room. It was tidy and spotless. I couldn't tell if there were any children in the family.

"*Bambino*s?" I asked her, before realizing that I was speaking the Italian I had learned from my childhood friends.

"*Dos*," she smiled proudly, obviously understanding me anyway. I presumed they must be in school since it was still early in the afternoon. Up close, Anna had high cheek bones and thick brown eyebrows. She looked to be in her early fifties. Although we were fairly close in age, she exuded a maternal quality that made me feel like a child again. Watching every move I made, I realized she was waiting for me to take a sip of coffee so I raised the bowl to my lips, hoping it wasn't too hot. It was delicious, perfectly creamy with a hint of coffee. I nodded my head in approval. She broke into a proud smile wnd using her hands she encouraged me to drink more.

Anna reminded me of my childhood Italian friend, Lucy, whose mother used to feed me every time I visited her house. The food was so good that I always ate more than I should have. With seven children in our family there was often not enough food for seconds, so I wasn't accustomed to eating until I was full. Lucy's mom would always say, "Lucy, why you no eat like Suzie?" Then she'd pinch my cheek until it hurt and offer me more home-made pasta, which I couldn't refuse.

Anna sat back in her chair, pleased that I was enjoying her offering. I took another sip, now self-conscious that she was watching so closely. My digestive system was lactose-intolerant but I kept drinking because I didn't want to be disrespectful. Besides, it was like getting comfort and nourishment all at once and it tasted so good that I decided it was worth any possible side effects later. I broke a long silence by telling her I was on my way back to Santiago and asked how far it was to the top of the mountain that I could see from her village.

"*Quando kilometres a la montange?*" I blurted out, surprising myself with my Spanish accent.

"*Dos kilometres,*" she said and pointed up the mountain. She somehow explained to me that I should turn right at the top of the mountain—*a derecho*—and follow that road down to the next village. She sat on the edge of her chair waiting to respond to my every need.

It was a beautiful example of how villagers along the Camino serve the needs of pilgrims who are strangers, without question or expectation. There was a natural maternal desire among the women to nurture. I thought about my Dad's mother, Evelyn Regan, who was the proprietor of a variety store on Rogers Road in Toronto. After my grandfather died, she worked seven days a week,12 hours a day for over 30 years. She taught me about serving people by her example during the daily interactions with her customers. She used to treat every customer equally. As a teenager, I worried that people would take advantage of her and some of them did. She was robbed three times, once at gunpoint. She finally sold the store when she was 73 years old. Walking this Camino route reinforced that my grandmother's intention to serve the needs of people without judgment, was an honourable and proud way to live. I wanted to be both more like my Grandmother and the women who I'd met on the Camino by serving complete strangers, without expecting anything in return. I finished my café and thanked her again for her generosity.

"*Gracias,*" I said bowing forward in honour. Through her example, I was reminded of a Camino lesson I had learned before; when a gift is received, a gift is given. Then, just like my mother did when I went off to school, Anna stood in the doorway and waved goodbye. There was a fine, misting rain as I headed up the mountain. The climb was steep and followed a road cut through a forest. Thankfully, the path was easy to follow. I got to the top of the mountain and looked for a sign. I saw a yellow arrow and it was pointing to the left. It was so familiar and comforting to me that I naturally followed it downward. I could see a village in the valley below and a shimmering river in the distance. I didn't recall seeing a river on the map, but then again the one I was using was very poorly drawn.

After walking downhill for almost an hour, my sand-filled blisters flared up again. I was tired and now very anxious to get to the next village. I kept looking for the city of Negreira in the distance but the only thing I could see was the farmer's fields. The villages in this part of Spain were all starting to look the same. I was almost at the bottom of the mountain when I spied a farmer standing in his field near the road.

I pointed to the village and in a questioning tone I said, "Negreira?" He solemnly shook his head and pointed to the top of the mountain. Why was he pointing that way I wondered? It was obvious he had misunderstood me since I was just up there so I repeated my question. This time I was careful to say, "Camino de Santiago," and I pointed to the village. Again he pointed to the top of the mountain.

"*Sí*. Camino de Santiago," he repeated.

I was sure that he understood me now, but I couldn't fathom why he was pointing in the direction I had just come from. I thanked him and continued walking down the mountain anyway. As I continued on my descent, I looked for another sign and soon discovered one right in front of me. It was a yellow arrow to Fisterra, where I had just come from. It was pointing down the mountain in the direction I was walking. Then it hit me. At the top of the mountain I'd turned left instead of right—*a derecho*—by following the direction the yellow arrow pointed, instead of going the reverse way I had retraced my steps. Inadvertently, I'd come back down the mountain and ended up in the very same village where Anna lived. Four kilometres up and down the mountain and I had discovered, I'd gone around in a circle.

Feeling sick at the prospect of walking up the mountain again, I had no desire or energy left. I sat down and cried again. When there were no more tears left, I stood up and waited for a car to come by deciding to get a ride back over the mountain. Half an hour passed and still none came. With no other option, but optimistic that I was back on the right path, I began the ascent up the imposing mountain for a second time. About half-way up a car approached and I waved to the driver to stop. It was a man driving the car.

"*Hola*," I said smiling as he opened the car window. He seemed friendly. "Do you speak English?" I asked. Thankfully, he did and he agreed to give me a lift to the next village over the mountain. Feeling safe with the stranger, I got in, unperturbed about riding part of the way in a car since I had already walked it once.

23

Village Encounter

The next day after I'd been walking for a couple of hours, I stopped to rest in a bus shelter in the village of Trasmonte. Seeing a man passing by, I stopped him to ask where there was a café and to my surprise, he also invited me to his home. Under normal circumstances, I'd never, ever, go with a stranger, especially a man, but because I was carrying the Eagle Feather and I was a pilgrim, I felt protected. Like Carlos had advocated, this was another chance to trust in the goodness of strangers on the Camino and so far with people like Anna, it had turned out well. Gratefully but with a little trepidation, I accepted his kind offer.

He led me to a quaint home on the main street of town. Just as we got there, a small white bakery truck stopped in front of the house and the driver bought out a tray of freshly backed bread and chocolate-filled croissants. The driver sold a stick of bread and a few croissants to the man and then flashed a warm smile my way. Despite my trust in the Camino's protection, I felt safer now that the bread man had seen me with this stranger. If something did happen, the police would be able to trace me back to here.

The man opened the door to his house and I was relieved to see a stout middle-aged woman standing there. Seeing that I was a pilgrim, she smiled warmly and welcomed me into their home. She insisted I sit at the table while she busied herself making coffee. Their names were Marisha and Daniel and they were brother and sister. Marisha told me she had a son who wasn't there at the moment. We talked about the Camino and Marisha happily moved around the kitchen. It was obvious they respected pilgrims and like so many others, they wanted to serve too. The proof of which was soon in front of me: a plate of the chocolate croissants fresh from the bread man himself. They served me coffee and about twenty minutes later I decided to leave.

While I was putting on my boots, they got ready to leave as well. Once outside, Daniel motioned for me to follow him. We went down the side street where a young man stood outside a garage. They spoke with such familiarity that I correctly guessed he was Marisha's son. Daniel opened the garage door and with obvious pride pointed to a small car. I didn't recognise the make but it looked like a typical European compact car. Daniel backed the car out while Marisha and the young man waited with me. I got the impression they were all going for a drive. Daniel jumped out of the car and opened the door for me. I shook my head to let him know I didn't need a ride.

"No. *Gracias,*" I pointed to my watch to let him know I wanted to walk and it was getting late. It was no use. Marisha motioned for me to get in the car too.

"*Misa, misa,*" she said repeating the word for Mass. Then I understood that they wanted me to attend Mass with them. After the warmth of their hospitality I couldn't refuse. We got into the car and drove only 750 metres down the road to a church. Daniel parked right up to the front entrance where we all got out. It appeared the whole village was standing outside and most of the women were dressed in black. They reminded me of the Italian women at my friend Pat's funeral before I left home. I wondered, how many months or years did they wear black to mourn a death? The villagers watched with curiosity as I emerged from the car. Marisha stood by me proudly and we walked arm-in-arm toward the group of women. They each kissed her on each cheek and then she introduced me as the Canadian peregrina, Susannah. I felt proud to be there with her. Most references to pilgrims are lumped into the masculine Spanish word peregrino. Since peregrina is the term used for a female pilgrim, hearing it gave me a new appreciation for the uniqueness of female pilgrims.

The Baroque-style church was named Iglesias Santa Maria. It was simply designed with rows of pews on either side. Oddly, all of the village men sat on the right side, while the women sat on the left. I followed Marisha to the front of the church and into the pew on the left again. Coincidently, the left side of our bodies represent the feminine side. The children gathered on the steps in front of the altar. My feet were aching so I surreptitiously took the opportunity to slip off my boots.

There was a tap on my shoulder. When I turned around a woman greeted me in English. We had a very brief conversation and then a hush came over the congregation as Mass began. The priest entered and everyone stood. At the side of the altar a nun played guitar while a small group of children seated around her sang a hymn. On the center of the altar, there was a statue of the Virgin Mary in a black velvet dress, holding a rosary. Beside it, there was another statue of the Virgin Mary dressed in blue with a golden halo over her head, her hands outstretched with children sitting all around her as though they were receiving a lesson. I wondered if she was teaching them about serving.

Even though I didn't understand Spanish, I could follow the familiar ritual of the universal Roman Catholic ceremony. When it was time for Communion, each aisle rose in turn and walked to the front. When it was our turn, I realized that I didn't have time to put my boots back on. I went forward in my socks, hoping I wasn't being disrespectful. As I approached the altar, I put my hand on the Eagle Feather under my clothes, feeling comforted that it was with me. The sacrament of Communion was given in the old-fashioned way. The priest held the host up and spoke a few words in Spanish. He placed the host directly on my tongue and after I blessed myself with the sign of the cross I returned to my seat. It was evident the entire congregation was studying every move I made. At the pew I knelt down and said a prayer of thanks.

When Mass was over, the nun played the guitar and the children sang joyfully as we all filed out of the church. Outside I thanked Marisha for her generous hospitality. I found Daniel with a group of men and I asked him to point me in the direction of Santiago. Then I waved goodbye to Marisha and the entire congregation waved back with her. It felt like I was leaving my home. I walked away completely filled with unconditional love.

With renewed sense of hope, I walked through the village and I passed a single story building with a white picket fence. Celtic-sounding music was coming from inside and I stopped to listen. Impulsively, I opened the gate and walked up to the door. I knocked, but no one answered so I pushed it open. Poking my head inside the room, I looked around.

"*Hola*. Is anybody here?" Three men and a young woman turned around and motioned for me to come in.

"*No hablo Espanol*," I admitted and then introduced myself, "Me, Susannah from Canada."

One of the men said his name was Antonio and introduced each of them, saying their names as he pointed them out. Two of them were named Jose and one was the father of Alicia, a young woman holding a tambourine. She appeared to be very shy. Slender with pale white skin and black shoulder length hair tied in a ponytail, she looked to be about sixteen years old. They said that Antonio was the maestro of the group. I urged them to resume playing music by doing a little impromptu jig on the spot. They all laughed and began to play their instruments.

The music had a delightful medieval Celtic sound. The young woman tapped out a quick, rhythmic beat on the tambourine while I kept time with my walking stick on the hardwood floor. The older Jose played a wooden flute and the tune reminded me of the theme from a favourite childhood TV show, *The Friendly Giant*. The younger Jose played a small bagpipe as did Antonio. I admired him for spending time playing music with his daughter. It was an experience I never had with my father. Not that he ever played a musical instrument, but with seven children there was only so much time to spend with each of us. One of my fondest childhood memories is of being alone with my Dad when he took me out for my first steak dinner at a restaurant to celebrate my thirteenth birthday.

Without warning, the older Jose grasped my hand and we started to dance. With our arms locked, he swung me—and my backpack—around the room. It was a long and lively song and by the end of it I was out of breath. Thanking them again I said good-bye and set out on the path. I walked out of the village and onto the road that went gradually straight downhill for about five kilometres. As soon as I saw a stone I picked it up and carried it for a while. At the bottom I arrived at a village called Aquapesada and as usual there was a bar. Inside, I was confronted by a room full of loud men all smoking and drinking. It was soccer season in Spain and there was a game on the TV mounted over the bar. As one, they all turned and looked at me. I nodded and walked past them to the washroom. When I returned, I chose a table near the front door. I took off my boots and went up to the counter to buy some orange juice.

A TV commercial was playing. I read about it on a Camino list serve it was filmed in Obradoiro Square in Santiago. A popular soccer star kicks a ball around the square and then a monk appears unexpectedly and catches the soccer ball in mid-air. In the commercial, the monk looks at him sternly and then leaves, taking the soccer ball with him into the Cathedral. Apparently, during the taping of the commercial, the soccer player had accidentally kicked the ball through one of the huge stained glass windows of the Cathedral. He personally paid to have the window repaired and because of his fame, the story made headlines throughout Spain and Europe. At the end of the commercial, I laughed out loud, both at the ad itself and at the idea of yet another monk figuring into my journey.

Instinctively, I looked around the room to see who else found it amusing. The wall of solemn-faced men suddenly broke into broad smiles at me and one of them raised his glass in a toast. In turn, I saluted him with my orange juice and then the entire bar full of men hoisted their drinks. I felt like one of the boys.

24

A Pilgrim Meal

Late the next day, physically exhausted but spiritually invigorated, I arrived in Santiago for the second time on this journey, still in possession of the Eagle Feather. After a walk around Obradoiro Square, I went back to see if I could get a room at the hostel I'd stayed at before. Only a week had passed but it seemed like a much longer time ago. For only fifteen Euros, the same man gave me a double bed in a room that faced the street, instead of the over-sized closet. He generously offered to buy me vinegar and sea salt again. Grateful for his offer, I accepted.

After a long warm bath, I changed into semi-clean clothes, locked the room and went back to the Parador Hotel, where Judith had stayed. Longing to experience another tradition of the pilgrims of the past, I went to the reception desk and inquired about the free pilgrim meal that was offered. This thirteenth century building was once a pilgrim's hospital. Since they only served a maximum of ten people at each meal, I wanted to get there early. The clerk told me to take my Compostela certificate with me to prove I was a pilgrim and go to the underground parking lot to register with the attendant there.

When I arrived, there was only one other pilgrim waiting. He introduced himself as Oliver, from Normandy, France. He had a rugged face and wild gray hair that stood out all over his head. Although he was French, he reminded me of a fierce-looking Viking warrior. Another French pilgrim named Delores arrived and at exactly 7:00 p.m. we were all escorted through the parking garage, across a courtyard, into the luxury hotel and through the back entrance of the kitchen. One of the waiters handed each of us a tray, a large dinner plate heaped with meat, vegetables and potatoes and a basket of bread. We helped ourselves to complimentary water, wine, and fresh fruit. We were directed to a special dining room for the pilgrims downstairs. The walls were decorated with wood-framed old maps of the various Camino routes. Through the open window we could hear the activity of people going about their daily lives outside.

We said grace together and then Oliver immediately started telling us about his adventurous life. He'd recently sold all of his worldly belongings and expected to be wandering as a pilgrim on the road for the next two years. I was thankful for the little high school French I knew since it helped me to talk about my journey and tell the story of the Eagle Feather. They were fascinated to hear about our Canadian Native folklore. Dolores didn't say much but Oliver's engaging personality kept us laughing. Fortified by the meal and the hospitality, we returned our trays to the kitchen and agreed to meet for breakfast the next day. Alone again, I sauntered around the streets admiring the buildings and embracing the mystical ambience of this great holy city.

25

Touching the Eagle Feather

The next morning, I soaked my feet and did some blister surgery, well aware that I still had another one hundred and twenty-five kilometres to walk back to Portugal over the next six days. I packed my things and again left my backpack locked in the room. On the way to meet Oliver and Delores for breakfast, I re-visited the Cathedral for the last time. Entering the Portico de la Gloria, I stopped to admire the iconography of Saint James and his two disciples. I was told that the figure of Saint Susannah was amidst their statues. I wondered what fears she had to face to achieve sainthood.

Walking up the main aisle, I heard the faint murmurs of prayers being said all around me. In front of the impressive Baroque-style high altar I genuflected and blessed myself as a sign of respect. Walking to the left, I crossed the marble floor past the huge pillars that surrounded the altar. Prior to leaving on this journey, I had invited my friends and family to send me their personal intentions. I made a promise to carry them with me on my journey to Santiago. Before leaving, I had read each intention out loud, putting them into a stone just like I had done so many times with my sorrow. That day, I said a special prayer for all the intentions to be heard. I placed the stone on a ledge so they would be near the Saint. Then I walked through the familiar entrance to the *confessio* that held the remains of the Apostle.

After Saint James was beheaded by King Herod, his body was sent on a ship back to Spain where it was buried near the city of Padron and forgotten for several hundred years. Roughly 600 years later they were discovered by a hermit who had received a message from God instructing him where to find them. The remains were brought to Santiago to be eternally venerated. Not surprisingly, a theory disputing the idea that these are in fact the remains of the Apostle has arisen. For me, it was no longer about whether the legend of Saint James was true or false, right or wrong. It was like the story of the Sorrow Stones and had survived the test of time because people had faith and they believed it was so. In the end, even the legend of Christianity is just a story.

Passing through a low arched doorway, I stepped onto the noticeably worn-down marble stairs that lead to the crypt. I thought about the millions of pilgrims who had walked this way for hundreds of years before me. Through the narrow stone opening, I heard the voices of young boys singing, a heavenly sound that reverberated throughout the sacred space and raised goose-bumps on my arms. They sang in perfect harmony and with obvious devotion. Walking slowly with my head still down and listening attentively, I bumped into Oliver standing at the doorway.

"*Comment ca va,*" he whispered.

"*Ca va bien, merci. Et vous?*"

"*Bien, bien. Regardez,*" he said pointing to the entrance of the Saint's tomb. There was a velvet covered kneeler in front of the entranceway. The wrought iron gate, which usually kept the public from getting within three metres of the tomb, was wide open. I knelt down, bowing my head in thanks and praise for this special moment. Unconsciously drawing from my Roman Catholic upbringing, I blessed myself and began whispering the Hail Mary.

Beside the ornately carved silver casket, a priest began saying Mass in Spanish to a choir of young boys, who looked to be part of a school tour. I joined in following the familiar ritual. When the priest celebrated the consecration of the body and blood of Jesus, I watched closely as each boy received Communion. They didn't take the host in their hand. Just like at Marisha and Daniel's small church, they received the host in their mouth. When the priest finished giving them Communion, he beckoned me to come forward to receive the sacrament as well. I stood up from the kneeler and looked over to Oliver, hoping he would join me, but he was gone. I was the only outsider there. It was my own private pilgrim's Mass.

With trepidation, I stood and clasped my hands together resting them over the Eagle Feather. I stepped around the kneeler and walked forward knowing I had been personally invited inside the very sanctum that housed the sacred remains of Saint James, the Apostle. I remembered that the pilgrims of the past believed if they were close to the remains of a Saint, they would be closer to God. Each step forward, took me closer to God and further back into the history of the story being created at that moment. It was as if everything that was happening was moving in slow motion.

Stepping onto the beautifully designed marble floor, I tentatively approached another arched passageway that led into the tomb. Nervously, with my head bent forward and my hands clasped together in prayer, I drew nearer. The silver casket itself was surprisingly small and rested on a platform about waist height. The priest stood next to it in his ceremonial robe, holding a chalice in front of him. As I stood before him, he offered me the body of Christ, holding the host in front of me. Lifting my head up, I opened my mouth and tipped my tongue forward in time to receive the offered host as he placed it there. It was wet, soft and it didn't stick to the roof of my mouth like the dry stiff host I was used to receiving at home. Automatically, I blessed myself by making the sign of the cross. I quickly swallowed the host and returned to the kneeler, where I said a prayer of thanks. The priest gave everyone a blessing and I watched as the choir boys tenderly touched the casket and then blessed themselves with the same hand. When the priest finished saying Mass, the choir of young boys gathered around the casket and began singing a hymn. The priest invited me to come up again. He beamed beatifically as he watched me move closer, then he gently stepped to the side.

With the reverence one would approach God, I walked slowly, moving forward in time with the tempo of their singing. Now that I was up close to the casket, I could see the detail of the Christogram—the Greek symbol of the name *Christ*—carved on the lid. It sparkled brilliantly in the light. Just as I was about to touch the casket, an overwhelming sense of fear came over me. I knew I was as close as anyone was going to get to venerate the physical remains of Saint James. I was paralysed and suddenly uneasy with being so near to God. Feeling out of control, I was tempted to just turn around and run away. The hymn ended and the room went silent. All I could hear was the sound of my own heart beating.

Tenderly, I rested my left hand over the place where I was keeping the Eagle Feather of the Creator. Tenderly I placed my right hand on the cold silver casket of the Apostle of God. Closing my eyes, I opened myself to receiving all of the love of the Creator and God. Within seconds, I was filled with immense joy and a feeling of divine love flowed through every cell of my entire being. I held my breath—in a state of utter ecstasy—not wanting the moment to end. The place where my hand rested on the casket became warm. I bowed my head forward. My hand ran along the edge of the ornately carved lid to the corner and slipped down the side of the casket. Standing there in a state of grace, I thanked God for giving me the courage to walk the steps of the pilgrims of the past. By touching the remains of the Catholic Apostle Saint James, like the pilgrims of the past, I believed I had been closer to the almighty power of God. By carrying a sacred Native Eagle Feather, I believed I was connected to the Creator. As a pilgrim on the road to Santiago, I believed that the Camino had connected us all.

26

A Dark and Stormy Night

It had been pouring rain for hours. I walked alone along the side of a busy highway, constantly splashed with waves of mucky water by cars speeding by. My Gore-Tex jacket leaked and I was soaked to the skin. The nylon rain pants I wore were drenched and sticking to my slightly damp hiking pants. My boots were sopping wet and my socks were sodden too. I'd lost my poncho and I hadn't seen a store for hours. My backpack grew heavier as it took on water. There was no where to go to escape the downpour and the day's weather forecast was calling for more of the same.

After crossing a stone bridge painted a bright turquoise blue color, I rounded a bend and finally saw the village of Teo. I crossed the street and went into a bar hoping to dry my clothes and find directions to the albergue. It was a dirty, noisy place with old faded travel posters on the wall and a cooking pan full of home-made Spanish *empanada* sitting uneaten on the counter. It was a tired old building that had probably been a bar for a very long time. Tables and chairs lined the walls with a long counter across the back of the room. The requisite television set above the bar, blared a sports program.

It was difficult communicating with the grizzled owner because of my negligible Spanish and his impenetrable rural accent. I couldn't tell whether he said the albergue was two hundred metres or two kilometres away. He handed me a card with a phone number of the hospitalero. The bartender picked up the phone, dialled the number and handed me the receiver without saying a word. I heard a woman answer.

"*Hola,*" she said suspiciously, like she was asking a question.

I responded quickly, "*Buenos tardes. Hospitelero por favor?*" She grunted and then dropped the phone with a bang. There was prolonged silence. I waited. In the background I heard footsteps approaching and a male voice spoke into the phone.

"*Hola,*" a voice said. I paused, unsure of what to say. Pilgrims simply ask for help when they are lost, hungry, injured, or in need of a place to sleep.

"*Me peregrina. Qui albergue de peregrina?*" I asked hoping he would understand me. There was no response. Then the phone went dead. I waited, holding the receiver to my ear hoping someone would speak. There was only silence. I tried to remember what being on-hold sounded like in Spain but I couldn't recall. Finally, after waiting for what seemed like several minutes, I realized that he'd hung up the phone. Trying not to look stupid in front of the bartender, I mumbled something into the phone and put the receiver down. The bartender nodded and I thanked him, acting as if everything was fine. I returned to my seat not sure if hospitalero was coming to the bar or not.

Not wanting to take the chance of missing him, I quickly gathered my things and rushed outside. There, across the road, was a sign that said the albergue was indeed two hundred metres away, straight downhill from there. I was wet and freezing cold but knew I'd soon be warm and comfortable, so I tolerated it. Almost running down the hill, my backpack bouncing against my lower back, I finally found the albergue on my right.

It was a gorgeous stone building with bright yellow window frames and stood alone, nestled in the forest with no houses or other buildings near it. There was a covered patio with a clothes-line under it. Beneath the shelter of the overhang, I dropped my pack and began rooting for dry clothes to change into. I pulled off my jacket, rain pants and boots. Then clumsily I peeled off my fleece liner, shirt, hiking pants and, finally, my socks. I was standing outside almost naked except for my sports underwear, micro-fibre vest and a lot of goose-bumps.

Shivering uncontrollably, I pulled on a dry fleece top and some only slightly less damp pants from my backpack. I put on my last pair of dry socks and slipped into my boots without doing them up. I hung my wet clothes on the line to dry. My nose was running and I had developed an annoying cough. With my asthma, I was constantly worried about getting a cold that could move into my lungs. While waiting for the hospitalero to arrive, I was worried about what might happen and paced back and forth to keep warm while the rain poured down around me. What if no one showed up? Where would I sleep that night?

At least an hour went by and still no one came. I was now shaking uncontrollably from the damp and cold. My cough had worsened and completely exhausted, I slumped down with my back against the stone wall and re-considered my options. I could stay there and wait or I could begin walking to the next private hostel ten kilometres away. I decided to leave my pack there and walk back to the bar at the top of the hill. I thought maybe the hospitalero had arrived at the bar already and didn't know where I was. Maybe there was someone there who spoke English. Maybe they could help me. Maybe, maybe, maybe.

Wheezing from my asthma after the steep climb, I stepped inside the warm bar. The smoky air burned my weakened lungs. The sounds of a soccer game blared from the TV. The bartender was totally engrossed in the game. Leaving my wet poncho at the door, I walked up to him and excused myself for interrupting. I tried to explain that the hospitalero hadn't arrived and I needed to call him again. Without saying a word, the bartender pointed to a man at the bar who was watching the game. I walked over to him.

"*Hola.*" I said firmly, bending forward to put my face up close to him.

"*Una momento,*" he said, without turning to look at me. I was furious. He lifted his beer to show me that he still had a quarter of a glass left to drink and went back to watching the game. I tried not to react. It appeared that most of this time he'd been sitting at the bar, while I was freezing cold waiting to get inside the albergue. I wondered why he would act this way? Many of the people in the albergues along the way volunteered their time and I felt as a pilgrim, I didn't have a right to complain. But if someone decided to be a hospitalero as a vocation, I assumed it came with certain responsibilities to the pilgrims they chose to serve.

I stood right beside him, still shivering uncontrollably from the cold and started tapping my foot on the wood floor to get his attention. Unperturbed, he finished his beer, got up and left without saying a word to me. I followed him and he motioned me to get into his car which was awfully dirty and messy. I caught myself judging again. I looked for the seat belt but there wasn't one. He started the car and it made a loud rattling noise when he kicked it into reverse. During the short drive back down the hill to the albergue he said nothing.

At the albergue, feeling at ease now that I had a place to sleep, I took my boots off and stuffed them with newspaper to help dry them for the next day. I looked around the room thankful to see at least it was clean. A set of wooden stairs went up to the dorm. Off the main room, there was a kitchen with a long wooden table and eight chairs around it. The hospitalero started giving me instructions in Spanish. Exhausted, I barely pretended to listen. He told me the background and history of the building. I had no trouble understanding him when he proudly explained the new heating system that heated the floor of the building. He unexpectedly became talkative and even pleasant but I just wanted to go to bed. While he talked, I unpacked my wet clothes and laid them out all over the heated floor to dry. He went back to his desk and busied himself with paperwork. Hungry and thirsty, I knew I was almost out of food so I checked to see if there was anything in the kitchen to eat. I found hot chocolate in the cupboard and a package of cookies I assumed were left by previous pilgrims. Grateful, I plugged in the kettle and opened the package of cookies using an enormous butcher knife I found out on the counter. While waiting for the kettle to boil, I approached his desk and presented my credential. He noted the details of my name, age, country, passport number and the place where I started my pilgrimage in the registration book. I assumed that he could tell I was walking *sola*. He picked up a small metal box marked *Donativo* and deliberately set it in front of me.

Some of the albergues in Galicia ask for a donation and it's expected that pilgrims pay whatever they want although the average is around three Euros. Conscious of the cookie in my hand and the warm floor under my feet, I put five Euros in the box, he smiled and nodded his head slightly with approval. He stamped my pilgrim credential and then he got up to leave. In a mix of English and Spanish, he warned me to lock the door and not let anyone in. I understood him to say that he wasn't expecting any more pilgrims that night because of the bad weather. He left and I heard the distinctive rattle of his car as it climbed the steep hill back to the bar.

It was getting dark out. I sat in silence at the kitchen table soaking my feet in the vinegar and sea salt solution, attempting to read some brochures in Spanish. The uncontrollable shivering had finally stopped but my face felt flushed, like I had an unusually high temperature. Outside the window, I could see there was nothing but the foreboding silhouette of the shadowy forest. I was completely alone.

I spent some time writing in my diary, but the chills had returned and I decided go to bed early. With the lights out, I reasoned that a stranger coming by would simply assume that the albergue was closed and move on. Stepping around my clothes that were laid out on the floor, I went upstairs and chose a top bunk near the heater. Stripped down to my underwear and micro-fibre vest, I crawled happily into my sleeping bag grateful to be dry and warm. Rain pounded on the roof. I lay very still, feeling mentally and physically exhausted. Perhaps selfishly, I was thankful that I still had the Eagle Feather with me for protection.

"*Miigwech Creator*," I said to myself tucking it inside my sleeping bag and feeling safe in its presence. To distract myself from my fears, I planned the next day in my mind. Since I hadn't reached Padron today, I'd have to make up an additional eleven kilometres tomorrow. I quickly fell into a dream-filled sleep.

A bell rang. I bolted upright. It sounded like the doorbell of our old home on Prince Edward Drive in Toronto. Looking around, it slowly dawned on me where I was. It was still raining hard. I heard thunder and then, a loud banging on the door. A voice called out. It was a man's voice. Fighting confusion and panic, I knew I had to protect myself. My heart raced. I tried to remember where I left my Swiss Army Knife but it was dark. Then I remembered seeing a butcher's knife in the kitchen downstairs. I slipped out of the bunk bed quietly and crept down the stairs. I didn't turn on the lights so I would be able to see who was lurking there before he could see me. He rapped on all the windows along the front of the building. Then he banged on the front door, then the side door, frantically calling out. I wanted to call the police, but the only phone was a payphone and it was outside.

Bang. Bang. Bang.

I didn't know what to do. I hid in the shadows and then crept into the kitchen. Perhaps if I could see him I would know what to do. I waited in the dark, my heart beating loudly, I shivered standing in my sports underwear and a sleeveless vest.

Bang. Bang. Bang.

Then I saw him. His face lit faintly by the security light and barely recognisable. He looked like an evil villain with a staff and a huge dark cape that was flapping in the wind. All I wanted to do was hide in the dark until he gave up and left. I didn't want to have to decide whether to let him in or not.

Bang. Bang. Bang.

The stranger stepped into the light and I could see the desperation in his eyes. He was obviously wet from the torrential rain. His face was pressed up to the glass and his eyes darted around the room. Water dripped from the hood of his poncho onto his wet face. I strained to see what he looked like asking myself if I could really decide whether to help someone not by their looks?

Bang. Bang. Bang.

There was a loud crash of thunder and then a bolt of lightning filled the main floor of the albergue with light. In that split second, he saw me. Our eyes connected. His pained expression pleaded with me to resist my fears but I was a woman alone. I felt weak and vulnerable standing there, exposed and almost naked. Then I wondered about his perspective. How could he possibly convince me that he meant me no harm?

Bang. Bang. Bang.

He pounded on the window again, calling out to me. I couldn't bear to watch him any longer. I walked over to the glass door, shaking with fear and crossing my arms to cover myself.

"Who are you?" I shouted.

"*Peregrino. Peregrino.*" I heard him say in a muffled voice. Of course he would say that, I thought to myself.

"Show me your Compostela," I yelled hoping at least his pilgrim credential would confirm he was a pilgrim and give me his name.

Somehow, I thought I'd feel safer just knowing who he was. He pointed to the bottom of his pack to let me know it was in there. Then he turned to show me the scallop shell crest on the back of his poncho.

"*Por favor,*" he pleaded, through the glass door.

How could I turn away a pilgrim in need? Then I thought that maybe this was a test for me, to see whether I could trust that the Camino and the Eagle Feather would really protect me. I had no idea who he was and why he was there so late at night. Regardless, I had to make a decision to let him in or not. Moving closer to the window I noticed that he wasn't much taller than me and I thought that would help if I had to defend myself.

Finally, I made the decision that I couldn't ignore him. He was a pilgrim in need. I turned the lock. The door burst open and the sound of wind and torrential rain filled the room. He stepped inside and I quickly shut the door behind him to keep it warm. Water dripped all over the floor leaving a puddle where he stood. He grabbed the edges of his rain poncho and peeled it off and then turned around to look at me. I immediately became self-conscious that I was standing there in my underwear.

"*Hola.* I'm Susannah, the Canadian," I said naively hoping to disarm him with the fact that I had both a saint's name and that I was from Canada. He stuck out his hand and introduced himself. His hand was wet and cold. I didn't hear a word he said since I was too busy judging his actions and watching for clues as to whether to mistrust him or not. I cautiously helped him remove his backpack and invited him in. I showed him the heated floors where he could lay his clothes to dry. Upstairs my hospitality ended when I directed him to a separate bunk room on the opposite side of the building from me. When I was safely back in my bed, I made sure the Eagle Feather was close to me in my sleeping bag and I thanked the Creator for protecting me. Even though I rationalized I was safe, I felt uneasy with someone else in the building. I laid there wide awake in the darkness, for what seemed like hours, listening to his restless movements on the other side of the room.

The next morning I got up early, packed and went downstairs to eat. I was enjoying some tea and an orange when the dishevelled pilgrim came down the stairs in his underwear and T-shirt. His name was Jose and he was a pilgrim from Portugal on his way to Santiago. He turned out to be friendly and kind-hearted, not threatening at all. When I finally I dared to look into his eyes, I realized I had nothing to fear. He was a pilgrim like me. He rambled on in Portuguese, perhaps because I nodded and smiled a lot he thought I could understand. He kept thanking me and bowing his head forward to show his appreciation for letting him in. He talked excitedly while helping me put on my backpack. We hugged, kissed on each cheek and said good-bye. All alone, I had faced my fear of being raped or murdered and now I felt completely at peace with myself. I had learned to trust.

Once outside, I looked back to see him standing in the doorway watching me walk away. Just before I was completely out of sight, I turned around and waved. He waved back.

27

Lessons from the Brits

When I walked the route towards Santiago, I asked for directions just by saying the word Camino like I was asking a question. The local people understood clearly and would point me in the right direction. On this return route, however, getting directions from Muxia was more of a challenge. The helpful villagers would often assume I was going in the wrong direction. After a few attempts at explaining that I was going in the reverse direction on purpose, I'd learned that if I said the words *returna de Camino* and at the same time I spin my forefinger in a circle to indicate that I was going around in a circle, they understood me.

It was now April 20th and I'd been walking for fifteen days, the last four in unremitting rain. I was feeling physically strong but very wet. Most of the time there wasn't anyone else walking on the path with me and this gave me the chance to spend time completely alone with myself. My patience was constantly tested by practising the discipline of surrender. If I could let go of my desire to control who would receive this great honour, I hoped it would open the possibility to attract what was needed. I was learning that I was only the messenger for the Creator, not the message itself and now I trusted the beneficiary would ultimately find me.

The rain stopped momentarily. I couldn't help but wonder if it would ever be dry enough to be dusty like in Sherry's dream. Setting my backpack down on a rock, I took the Eagle Feather out of its red cloth home. Holding it up to the sky, a feeling of immeasurable gratitude filled me. I was grateful for my legs, so I could walk; for my eyes, so I could see; for my voice, so I could speak; for my ears, so I could hear and for the Eagle Feather, so I could be a part of its sacred journey. After this prayer of thanks, I kissed the Eagle Feather and then spoke from a place of complete love and honour.

"*Miigwech Creator,*" I said proudly.

Arriving on a hilltop, I came upon the village of Rua de Francos where one of the oldest wayside crosses in Galicia stood. Nearby were the famous Gothic ruins of Castro Lupario; a pre-Roman enclave that originally housed the body of Saint James for several hundred years before it was moved to Santiago. I noticed there were blue arrows painted along the way going in the opposite direction of Santiago. These, I discovered, directed other pilgrims journeying south to the famous pilgrimage site of Our Lady of Fatima in Portugal. Fortunately, now I could follow them to Valenca, Portugal.

Soon I passed through the town of Faramello. It was downhill all the way back to the dreaded N550 highway where it felt like my life was truly at risk walking on the narrow shoulder of the road. The traffic whipped by at 120 kilometres an hour. Even as I faced imminent danger I completely trusted that I would be protected and guided by the Creator. Walking the return route, I was now more attentive to my surroundings and focussed on just being a messenger. Retracing my steps brought a vague sense of déjà vu. I was remembering all of my Camino experiences again, except from another perspective and in a different context. I followed the moss-covered stone walls and passed by the gardens and homes of the villagers, like I was winding my way through their history. Following the river Sar, I paused to listen to the soothing sound of the moving water. I walked further and came to the train tracks I'd crossed with the German pilgrim, Kiko, and the flame-haired peregrina with the sanitary napkins in her boots. It was like a mirror of life before me, from another perspective.

Nearing the town of Iria Flavia, I followed a plain cement walkway which led to a beautiful church called the Collegiate Church of Santa Maria de Iria. Named in honour of the Virgin Mary, this again was a testament to the depth of the devotion to her on the Portuguese Route. There was a cemetery next to the church and I wandered around reading the dates and names of the people who had passed on. Several of the sarcophagi dated back to the sixth century. This was also the place where the famous Spanish poet, Rosalia de Castro, was first buried when she died in 1885, before she too was moved to her final resting place in Santiago.

Leaving the church, I crossed the road and walked through a desolate industrial area that took me through the village of Perdona. Continuing past numerous hamlets, I crossed the Cesures Bridge to again arrive at the famous city of Padron. According to legend, the Barca de Pedra, the ship that transported St. James' remains from Jerusalem to Spain, was originally moored here.

I again crossed the familiar stone bridge over the river to the fountain in front of the Convent of O Carme. I went into the albergue next to the church to find it was empty except for a woman mopping the floor. She pointed to the sign-in book and encouraged me to register myself. This was the same place where I'd had dinner with Santiago, Alberto, Ana—from San Sebastian, and her husband. That's when the guys played with the breast-shaped cheese and we laughed our way through dinner. This time, however, I spent a quiet evening alone resting and writing in my journal.

Early the next morning I set out on the path alone following brass scallop shells imbedded in the sidewalks. At the fork in the road, I went right and this led me into a forest of gorgeous old chestnut trees. It was easier to follow the reverse direction of the yellow arrows because they were painted on wooden signs mounted high up on the trees.

On this return journey, I was relaxing more, trusting that everything would be alright. I found when I freely surrendered to the path, it filled me with a sense of absolute calmness and peace. After walking through a pine tree forest, I became even more introspective and walked without resistance. Then a sign said I was leaving Casa Iderique and it was back to the N550 highway again. The peace and quiet of the mystical forest and Mother Nature abruptly ended with the sound of highway traffic.

Crossing over the river Bermana, I entered into the city of Caldas de Reis, my destination for that day. I followed the yellow arrows and easily found the albergue next door to the church of Saint Thomas. I was reminded of the Good Friday procession I watched outside the albergue. It was an ancient building with arched windows, a high ceiling and gorgeous wooden stairs. This was the place where the two the robust Spanish women had served their husbands with a massage and then put them to bed.

The hospitalero arrived and he was an impeccably dressed, middle-aged man with thinning hair who ran the albergue like a tight ship. Without a word, he handed me a sheet in English to read. It said the albergue closed at 10:00 p.m. and that I must leave in the morning by 8:00 a.m. sharp. Stern faced, he stamped my credential with a loud thud, noted my particulars in the registration book, and then abruptly left.

I settled by myself in a small private room that held two sets of bunk beds. Although there was no hot water to shower with, there was a unique bidet. I don't know how many different kinds I've seen in my life, but I couldn't seem to figure out how to work this one. There was no heat in the building, either, and I couldn't find extra blankets anywhere, so I tucked my silk liner inside my sleeping bag and slept without moving. As the night passed, it got colder, as if the damp outside air seeped through the stone walls.

The next day with the efficient hospitalero standing by to make sure I left on time, I packed my things. It was just before 8:00 a.m. when I left and still dark so I had trouble finding the route markers. After almost an hour walking on the narrow shoulder of the N550 highway, the fumes from the diesel exhaust were making me feel sick. Again off the highway, I walked for about an hour without seeing a sign. It was raining hard, I'd put plastic bags inside my boots to keep my feet dry but with each step, I could feel my feet slipping, putting strain on my other muscles. I walked alone in silence. With each step, I tried to relax by following my breath and quickly moved into a meditative state. The muscles in my legs softened and I stopped resisting. I walked without thought, enjoying the wetness of the rain on my face. The colours around me appeared more vibrant and all of my senses were elevated to a state of ultimate clarity. Even the pain from my blisters was gone. I wasn't just walking on the Camino as a pilgrim, I was being the Camino as I walked.

I followed the pilgrimage to Fatima directional arrows that were painted blue, past farmer's fields and along the streets of the local villages. After walking through a forested area, I came across a community washing pool, a large shallow basin with a covered roof and open sides. Often I'd seen village women sitting around the edge of these pools, washing their family's clothes. At this one, two women were sitting talking. They were pilgrims.

"*Hola*," I called out, hoping they spoke English.

"*Hola*," one of them answered.

"Do you speak English?"

"Yes, we do," the same woman replied in a lilting British accent.

Then the other woman spoke. "I'm Lynn and this Rosemary. We're from England," she said. I was glad to meet them. Lynn appeared to be the more outgoing of the two and jumped into a conversation right away. She was the kind of person whose personality was revealed through everything she carried. I teased her about the two pairs of eyeglasses on chains that hung from her neck. She said she had the middle-aged challenge of not being able to see far away or up close either.

"I can only see in-between," Lynn said with a big smile, "and for most needs in life, it's quite useless." We all laughed with her. While Lynn spoke in generalities, Rosemary filled in the details. It was like talking to one person when they spoke. They told me they'd been friends for a long time and lived on neighbouring farms near the same village in the north of England. They were like an old married couple and had a routine with each other that had been refined over innumerable cups of tea and I loved being in their company.

My Mum always used to say you could tell a lot about a person by their shoes. I tried not to judge but I couldn't resist checking out Lynn's feet. They were huge, or at least her shoes were. She was wearing white runners or, as they call them in England, plimsoles. They were thin, made of canvas and offer absolutely no support. I wondered how she could possibly walk the Camino in them. Rosemary noticed me looking at Lynn's running shoes.

"She went to the camping equipment shop back home and bought a pair of leather hiking boots for one hundred pounds, only to find out they were quite useless." Rosemary said.

"She'd finally mailed them back home since they were nothing but trouble." Rosemary added.

"So, I bought these plimsoles," Lynn said proudly wiggling her clownish feet.

Rosemary piped in, "And believe it or not, they're two sizes too big and far more comfortable."

In addition to her remarkable shoes, Lynn had startling eyes. They were crystal blue and when she spoke, her long eyelashes fluttered with excitement. I could see a dark sadness in them and I made a mental note to pick up a stone for her on my way. This was Rosemary's first pilgrimage, but Lynn had walked part of it before with her twenty-eight year old son. She talked about how she'd struggled to integrate the Camino experience when she returned home.

"Lynn was very emotional and cried all the time for about six months afterward," Rosemary said. "We made a pact to walk the Camino together one day. And so here we are." They both looked at each other and laughed together.

I told them about my own difficult transition coming home and how after my first journey I'd decided to live the Camino everyday of my life. I had learned that walking was a state of being, not something to do. I wanted to be in this state everyday of my life. After the profound experience I had on the first journey, I decided that I wanted to live the Camino everyday. By telling my stories, I found I could relive my own journey over and over again. Sharing the simple pilgrim fables also opened up more possibilities for philosophical discussion, especially with complete strangers. By creating dialogue about the Camino as a metaphor for a life journey, I told them this was my way of giving something back to the Camino.

"But why are you walking the other way on the Camino?" Rosemary inquired.

"I made a promise to myself that I'd come back and walk the route in both directions, like the pilgrims of the past."

"What's it been like to walk backwards?" Lynn asked.

"Well, it gives me a different perspective about something I already know. It helps me to remember things I have forgotten or things I didn't know I knew. Walking back has reminded me who I am. Nothing about me has really changed, only the way I see myself is different."

Saying it out loud, I began to truly comprehend how the return walk had impacted my life. I was integrating the Camino lessons I'd learned while I was still on the path, instead of waiting until I returned home. I hoped that because of this any transitional at home would be easier this time.

Then I made an off-hand comment about the physical demands of walking with blisters and all the weight on my back, Lynn began instructing me on how to walk with a backpack. I wasn't sure what anyone could teach me about walking at this point, but I listened willingly.

"Right then, stand up. Let's give it a go, shall we?" Lynn gladly jumped into action and put on her backpack. Her backpack was very small and tightly packed. She had a large bag of chocolate chip cookies swinging from a string tied to a strap. Lynne confessed that she loved chocolate and this way she could easily reach for an instant fix if she had a craving while walking. Her camera was clipped onto the pocket of her hiking jacket on one side and a Swiss army knife hung from the other.

"The first thing to do," Lynn said, "is to be aware of putting all the weight you are carrying onto the entire area of the bottom of your feet. Imagine that you're flattening out your foot as you step down allowing the weight to evenly disperse."

"It's based on Tai Chi," Rosemary explained as she demonstrated. I was open to any suggestions so I tried it. Walking that way did feel lighter and more natural.

"Gently round your shoulders forward so they're in a relaxed state with your arms swinging in front of your body," Rosemary explained in her soft but commanding voice.

"I feel like a monkey," I said, laughing.

"And you look like a monkey," Lynn confirmed. "That's what you want."

"Lean into the backpack," Rosemary instructed, "and use your body weight to counter the weight of the pack and you'll see it gives you the feeling that you are carrying no weight at all." This time

Lynn demonstrated. She described the feeling of gently pressing my lower back into the base of the backpack, shifting the weight. I felt the difference right away. Not only did my pack feel weightless, but using the entire base of my foot to take on the weight lessened the pain in my blistered feet. It was working.

"It's taking the pressure off my feet." I said, practising it with them.

"Indeed, it's like having your own sherpa to carry the weight," Rosemary added.

"Have a cookie," Lynn offered, holding out the bag invitingly. I gladly took one and sat down. They started to get ready to leave.

"Before you both leave can I ask you something?" I said.

"Sure, love," they answered together.

"Do you know anything about the Native Eagle Feather?" They shook their heads.

"Never heard of it," Lynn said, "but it sounds simply fascinating. Why are you asking us?"

"On this Camino, I've been sent on a quest to share the stories of the Eagle Feather. Through a vision in a dream, I've been asked to give the Eagle Feather to a leader, someone who will honour the teachings of the Native people." I paused to wait for a reaction from them.

"That's remarkable. Who did you give it to?" Lynn said.

"No one yet. I haven't found anyone to given it to and now I'm afraid that I may have to take it home with me. My greatest reward is guarded by my greatest fear."

"Darling, you are your greatest reward," Rosemary said, putting her arm on my shoulder. "Just be yourself, love. The right person will come to you." Those were the words that I needed to hear. Again I was learning, I had to trust.

"Maybe the feather is for you, dear," Lynn blurted with excitement in her voice. She was right in a way. The quest of the Eagle

Feather was as much about the journey of my search for the recipient, as it was about the person who was to receive it.

"It's time for us to go now, Rosemary dear," Lynn gently reminded her. I was sad to leave them. I hugged each of them, awkwardly wrapping my arms around them and their backpacks.

"*Ultreya*," I said.

"Pardon me?" Rosemary asked.

"*Ultreya* is an ancient greeting for the pilgrims who walk to Santiago. It means onward in Latin." They listened with interest. "On their return journey from Santiago the pilgrims of the past were greeted with the word *suseya*. It means upward. So it was onward to Santiago and upward back home." After I said it to them out loud, I wondered if *suseya* meant that the pilgrim's journey back was upward, toward God or maybe the Creator.

"*Suseya*," Lynn repeated, then turned away to hide the emotional tears streaming down her face. She started to walk away.

"She's crying again," Rosemary said assuredly. "Don't worry, I have a tissue." They walked as one, serving each other's needs.

"*Ultreya*." I called out to both of them. I turned and started to walk again. With each step I took forward, I felt like I was walking back to myself.

28

Another Kind of Mission

I seemed to be on a constant downhill trek over rocks and mud with water flowing all around. It was like walking down a waterfall. I kept my head down, watching each step, careful to avoid a sprain on the slippery stones. I tried placing the arch of my feet on the rocks to keep weight off my newly-healed blisters. There was the sound of heavy breathing, coming closer. I looked up to see a man striding up the hill like he was climbing stairs three steps at a time. He was wearing shorts and immediately noticed the muscles rippling on his bare legs. It was obvious he was in great shape. He flashed his perfect white teeth with a big smile. I blinked my eyes to be sure he was real.

"*Hola*," I said noticing that he was very handsome.

"Do you speak English?" he asked with an American accent.

"Yes," I answered, still dumbfounded by his stunning good looks. I couldn't help staring at the chiselled bone structure of his face. He had short dark hair, lightly-tanned skin and a long straight nose. I guessed he was in his late twenties. I knew I was judging him by his looks, but I couldn't stop myself.

"My name is Phil. I'm from New York," he said and began to peel an orange. My hand went straight to the Eagle Feather nestled beneath my jacket. "Are you American?" he asked, looking me up and down as he dropped the peelings on the ground.

"No, I'm Canadian," I said while looking down at the mess he was making. I thought, at least it was organic.

"It's almost the same," he said popping an orange section into his mouth.

"No it isn't," I said somewhat defensively. He ignored my comment preferring to talk about himself.

"I was in the army," he said, taking another bite. "It's not something I'm proud of but it got me into fantastic shape." He kept eating and talking. "You see, I'm on a mission." He spoke with such confidence that if he'd also told me he was a spy, I think I would have believed him.

"What's your mission?" I asked thinking maybe we had something in common.

"I'm walking from Tui to Santiago in two days," he said proudly. I was convinced he was crazy. With my mother in mind I checked out his shoes. They were the latest high tech designed running shoes. There I was judging again. Then he opened his small pack, took out a power bar and began eating it while he talked.

"That's over one hundred and twenty kilometres. Are you crazy?" I asked.

"I'm trying to break a record," he said telling me that the guy who set the previous speed record for this distance was now sleeping with his ex-wife and this was his way of getting back. I thought how very American to retaliate by competing in a race—even though he'd already been beaten—just to prove a point. I felt sorry for him. Then he started running on the spot and then announced he had to keep moving so he didn't lose any time. He said bye and quickly ran off. I had to wonder if he was oblivious to any of the holistic, spiritual or religious benefits of walking the Camino path, let alone the life lessons he could learn from the pilgrims along the way. As I watched him run off, I finally stopped judging him, knowing he was on his own Camino. I trusted the Camino would provide everything that was perfect for him on his journey, whatever that might be.

29

The Final Days

The rain had finally let up and sunlight was bleeding through the trees of the forest. Listening to the transcendent sound of water, I felt like I was in a state of completeness. Taking a full breath, I lingered there and I smelled the natural woody scent of the forest, longing to remember it forever. Even though I still hadn't found someone for the Eagle Feather, I truly believed that my life was perfect and I had everything I needed. Everything except that when nature called, I often had to resort to peeing outside.

Feeling hungry, I sat down on my backpack and ate the rest of my *bocadillo*, a Spanish sandwich filled with chorizo and cheese I'd bought at a bar earlier in the day. Then I savoured the last piece of dark chocolate that Nathalie had given me and drank most of the water I had left. I got up and put my backpack on.

It was another warm day and I only had ten kilometers left to get to Pontevedra. I was enjoying the time alone. I had purposely slowed my pace considerably and was now walking about three kilometres an hour. It wasn't because of my blisters, they were healing and so was my knee; I was simply taking my time because I didn't want the journey to end. Trudging leisurely through the quaint town of Braga, church bells rang in the distance reminding me of when I heard bells playing Ave Maria, the same hymn I'd heard on my way to Santiago. At that time it had reminded me of Pat's funeral on the day I left on this journey, where I'd remembered it being played at my wedding and at my sister Donna's funeral. I was having memories of memories of memories.

The sign said the village church was called Iglesia Porsella. There was an old cemetery beside it. Looking around the side of the building, I saw a man hauling on the ropes that rang the church bells. He was dressed in dark clothes and hunched over as if clinging to the ropes for dear life. I'd seen him before at a different church a couple of weeks before. Looking up, I could see there was a stork's nest set in the corner of the tower and wondered how the birds could live so close to the pealing bells.

"*Buenos dias*," I said smiling warmly.

He looked over at me. "*Buenos*," he muttered and went back to his work. Each time he pulled, his body tensed and his face contorted as he swung the massive bells many metres above our heads. In broken Spanish, I asked him why he was ringing the bells that day. He said it was to honour the dead. He turned away and pulled on the thick rope one more time. That one was for Pat, I thought.

When he finished he turned to me, as if waiting for me to ask another question. There were dark circles around his eyes. How did he become the village bell ringer, I wondered? Was this his vocation in life? He certainly looked born to the part. I asked him where the albergue was and he pointed up a steep hill. Just as I turned to leave, he added that it was closed for the season. Then he shuffled off and went into the church. I returned to the path to begin walking to the next albergue.

It started raining again. Eventually I stopped at a bar to dry off, buy some juice and use the bathroom. The lady behind the counter gave me some *tapas*, a small plate of complimentary Spanish appetizers often provided in bars with a drink. I was so hungry I devoured them in no time. Seeing this, she smiled and set down another plate. After thanking her, I asked if I was going in the right direction to reach Pontevedra and she confirmed that I was. I left her a tip and set out on my journey again.

Another hour passed and I still hadn't met any other pilgrims. At one point I stopped to admire the sun as it lowered on the horizon and thought about how grateful I was to just be there. To be walking on the Camino. Sometime later I came to a roundabout and found a directional scallop shell sign marking the way to Santiago. Since I was on the reverse route, I went in the opposite direction. Nearing the train station, I recognized the albergue right away. A fence surrounded the property and, once again, I thought it odd to have so much security for a pilgrim lodging. It was late in the afternoon and I buzzed the intercom to get through the locked gate.

It felt like a lifetime since I'd been there. It had been crowded for Easter with mattresses all over the floor and pilgrims were sleeping everywhere. Now I was one of the few pilgrims there. The same kind hospitalera was behind the counter and she greeted me like an old friend. She showed me to the bunkroom and I picked the same bed I had before. I unpacked my things and went for a cold shower. I quickly got dressed and leaving my backpack there, I went to check out the city and have some dinner. When I got back I soaked my feet, had some tea and went to bed.

In the middle of the night, I sprung upright. The balls of my feet were throbbing in pain. I grabbed my flashlight and looked. A large flap of skin had peeled off my foot and had stuck to the lining of my sleeping bag. It had exposed an area, about the size of a silver dollar of wet pink open flesh. Grossed-out by the sight of it, I turned away and couldn't look at it again. I carefully slipped my foot back down to the bottom of the sleeping bag. I went to sleep trusting that the tiny stones that had lodged under my skin on the Costa da Morte, were working their way out. Relieved and somehow grateful, I fell into a dreamy asleep.

30

Dreaming Awake

Somewhere behind me, a man appeared. Although I couldn't see his face, I knew he was divinely beautiful. I was calm and patient, standing motionless with my back to him as the wind blew around us. His energy moved closer and he gripped my arm in his enormous hand. Tenderly but firmly, he held me still.

There was a brief pause. Although he didn't speak any words, I heard his voice and felt his love. He assured me that everything would be fine. I trusted him unconditionally. He leaned forward and as though brushing my cheek with a feather, he kissed me. It was so light I wasn't sure it was a kiss at all or that he had even physically touched me. There was a sense of peace all around. I knew without a doubt that he was a part of me and I was a part of him. I stood there immersed in absolute love as an eternal moment passed. I wanted to be with him forever. I wanted to know him in all ways. I turned around to tell him, but he was gone.

Desperate to know who the man in the dream was, I lay very still and held my eyes shut in case there was a chance this powerful dream would continue. When I was finally convinced it had ended, I opened my eyes. Blinking, I sat up in bed. It was 4:30 a.m. so I took out my diary and began to write down every detail so I wouldn't forget it.

Many aspects of this journey reminded me of being in a dream where familiar things seemed strange and the strangest things seemed commonplace. As I walked the return journey, I became more conscious of a mystical connection I had with the pilgrims of the past that was beyond words. Passing through a small village, I came upon three women standing by a stone fence that surrounded a house. They were picking oranges off a tree and filling a basket. I stopped to greet them and asked if they knew the way to the village of Mos. Before I left, a fellow pilgrim had given me the name of an English professor and his wife, who lived there and I wanted to stop at their home on my way through.

One of them, a tall, slender woman wearing a cotton house dress with an apron over it, picked six big oranges off the tree and gave them to me. I tried to return four of them, telling her it was too much for me to eat, but the woman insisted I take them all. I peeled and ate two of them right away, as if I hadn't seen food in months. While I was eating, the slender woman went over to the open kitchen window where a loaf of bread was cooling in the breeze. She broke it, giving half to me. I thanked her and the others for their generosity and continued on my way.

After following the reverse direction of the yellow arrows, I reached the N550 highway again. At a fork in the road, I turned left and soon came to a little chapel I recognized. It was the one with a statue of Santa Marta holding a stalk of wheat. The chapel was empty. I felt compelled to walk up to the front pew on the left, just like Mum made us do when we were children going to Mass. Kneeling down, I blessed myself and said a prayer of thanks. I loosened the deerskin tie and took the Eagle Feather out of its red fabric home. Holding it in my open palms in front of me, I honoured its presence.

"*Miigwech Creator,*" I whispered. Gently, I set the feather down on the pew beside me and looked up at the statue of Santa Marta to say a prayer. For the first time, I could see her more clearly. It wasn't a stalk of wheat in her hand, it was a feather. A sense of clarity overcame me. I knew for certain that the recipient of the Eagle Feather had already been decided. All I had to do was take the steps required to get it to them. The direction of my quest was suddenly crystal clear. The responsibility of selecting someone for the Eagle Feather was no longer a burden. I just had to be patient and trust in the Creator. I carefully wrapped the Eagle Feather in its home and tucked it in my pouch. Standing up, with renewed vigour, I tossed my pack over my shoulders, tightened the buckles and left the chapel. Thinking of the British pilgrims, I used the Tai Chi method of walking that they had taught me. There was a feeling of lightness, like I was floating along the path effortlessly.

Entering a mystical forest surrounded by pine trees, I trekked straight downward over rocks for at least five hundred metres. Then I sauntered along the cushioned forest floor on a path past moss covered rock and a peaceful stream. Crossing another gorgeous stone bridge at Pontesampaio, where Napoleon apparently suffered one of his greatest defeats in Galicia, I climbed a steep hill to end up back on a paved road that was cut along the edge of the mountain. It was dangerous on the cliff, but the view was worth every step.

Following the Roman Way, I passed through the city of Redondela and the albergue in the historic Casa da Torre building. I followed the blue arrows to the top of the mountain where the path abruptly ended. I looked behind me, hoping that I hadn't missed a sign. Before I made the long trek down the mountain again, I wanted to be sure I was going in the right direction. It was warm so I decided to stop for a rest.

Dust swirled around me. Standing proudly, I put my hand over the Eagle Feather and without saying any actual words, I spoke directly to it from my soul. I admitted that at first, I didn't believe I was the right person to decide who should be the recipient, especially when I set out on my journey and everything seemed to be going wrong. Because of this I had doubted myself. Sometimes I even questioned if I was truly in direct connection to the Creator because that belief was so foreign to me. However, because Sherry believed in me, I accepted this quest and had faith that I would be guided on the Camino to meet this challenge and I was.

Then I took the Eagle Feather out of the pouch around my waist and un-wrapped the deerskin tie. Taking it out of its home, I held it tenderly in my hand and smoothed its ruffled vanes. I sat down. We had become very close and I felt a deep sense of love and compassion in its presence. I knew that the Creator was listening to me, so I continued my intimate conversation saying there were times when the quest of deciding who should receive the Eagle Feather was a heavy burden. To gain control, I felt I needed to define the criteria. By setting standards, I was forced to judge people and situations. When I judged others, I closed all possibilities to be aware and I then didn't know what else to do. I was afraid of failing at my quest and that fear had paralysed me at times. When I had finally started to feel the connection to the Creator, selfishly I didn't want to give the Eagle Feather away because I was afraid to be alone without its protection.

I told the Creator through the act of being served by the unconditional kindness of people on the Camino, I felt a more profound compassion. Through compassion I learned that I was worthy. By being worthy, I had self-respect. Through self-respect, I was honoured as a pilgrim. By being honoured, I had faith. Through faith, I had surrendered. Through surrendering, I let go of control and I began to trust that it wasn't my responsibility to decide who should receive the Eagle Feather. I was only the messenger. I thought about how Sherry had remained open, trusting that she would know what to do with the Eagle Feather she had been given. Then unexpectedly, I had showed up in her dream proving in some way I had self-selected to be a recipient of the Eagle Feather as a part of its journey. Like the Eagle Feather itself, I was simply a vessel carrying a story and I knew didn't have to look for more answers out-side myself.

A circle was now complete.

Darkness was creeping in. I put the Eagle Feather away, slipped my backpack on and headed downward. Reaching the bottom of the mountain, I found an arrow pointing in the other direction. I hesitated. I didn't want to add extra distance to my already long day. A car came down the mountain road and I waved to the driver. Fortunately, he was very friendly and spoke some English. He told me that if I continued in the direction I was going over the moun-tain, I would eventually reach my destination. He offered me a ride. It was tempting but I thanked him and decided to walk. As he drove off I stood still, content to be listening to the sounds of the forest that wrapped around me. A church bell rang in the distance.

Climbing back upward, I reached the top of the mountain and recognised the beautiful Rosa granite picnic tables in the rest area. From there, I looked back reminding myself where I had come from. Following the blue arrows, I arrived in the tiny village of Mos. I stopped in the town bar and ordered a bottle of Apricot nectar. The helpful owner directed me to the home of the English professor and his wife who lived near the local school.

I knocked on the door and was greeted by a lovely couple. Both Adam and Theresa were thrilled to meet me and proudly intro-duced me to their son Daniel. After they served me Adam's home-made pizza, we sat around the table for most of the evening and talked. They kindly offered me a private room in a vacant furnished apartment next door, complete with a bath and hot water. After another evening of typically warm Spanish hospitality, I went to bed early taking the Eagle Feather with me.

31

Cafe con Leche at the Parador

It was the afternoon of my last day on the Camino. With renewed energy, I'd been walking for over six hours and had travelled twenty-six kilometres. That morning after I left Mos, I walked briskly along a stretch of industrial land to the bridge of San Telmo and ended up back on the boring path on the shoulder of the N550 highway for a long time. I was nearing the last leg of my journey crossing over the river Mino, back to the city of Valenca in Portugal, where I started.

While drinking a perfectly brewed *cafe con leche*, I gazed at the countryside through windows set in a stone wall half a metre thick. It was a million-dollar view of the river Mino for the price of a coffee. There were no screens on the windows and a warm breeze swept over me. No other people were in the café; only the two waiters who were serving me. I took off my boots and stretched my legs and the muscles in my feet.

The ceiling was made of wooden slabs with large beams set in a square design. The floor was built with wide pine tongue and groove planking. Floor to ceiling green and gold drapes framed the windows along two walls. I was sitting in an upholstered chair with a high stiff back and arm rests covered in red and purple fabric, resting in the luxurious lounge of another Parador Hotel in Tui. The building had been a pilgrim hospital at one time, but the only indication left was the napkins on the table: they were embossed with a scallop shell symbol and the words Ruta Jacobea—Route of Saint James.

Drawn to inspect the fabric on the chairs, I remembered being a child in Toronto when Portuguese immigrants arrived in our neighbourhood and some painted the outside brick on their homes in bright purple and red. My mother was appalled because she was very particular about matching colours. She taught us to co-ordinate our clothes and to never put purple and red together. The colour combination was foreign to me then, but having grown up in that neighbourhood, it now it seemed familiar and even pleasant.

An hour later and well-rested, I happily left the decadence of the Parador Hotel and found my way back to the simple pilgrim's path. It was late-afternoon and very hot. I had stripped off most of the layers of clothing I was wearing and since I didn't have any sunscreen, I could feel I was getting burned. There was road construction all around me and soon I was covered with a light film of dust. Since it was dusty, like in Sherry's dream, I wondered if the recipient for the Eagle Feather was nearby. I looked all around, but I was the only person there.

As I walked across the bridge over the river Mino, dividing Spain and Portugal, I looked far below me at the mighty water rushing by. Transfixed by the movement, I stood in a state of absolute presence and I promised the Creator that I would continue to share the stories of the First Nation people through the journey of the Eagle Feather, for as long as I lived. Turning to face Portugal, I started to walk forward, returning back to the very place where my journey had begun. Again I entered the tunnel that took me through the old fortress and followed the path that ended at the top of the hill. The sun was beaming onto the main street in Valenca where there was a bustling open marketplace.

32

Returning to Portugal

Walking through Valenca in a dreamlike state I found myself in front of the same linen shop where the taxi driver had dropped me almost three weeks earlier. It seemed like a lifetime had passed for me, but it was business as usual for the shop keepers. Looking in the window at the piles of beautiful linens, I saw a man working at a desk and woman folding material. I desperately wanted a picture taken here to signify the beginning and the end of this Camino. I went into the store and holding my camera up I said, "*Photographa por favor?*" The young woman stopped what she was doing, nudged the man standing next to her and pointed at me.

"Where are you from?" he asked, surprising me when he spoke English.

"Canada," I replied, still startled. He said that his name was George and he'd lived in Ontario for many years. He came outside and took a picture of me in front of his store. We talked about places he knew in Canada and then he offered to buy me a coffee. As we walked through the market, I told him I wanted to go to the Celtic people's settlement on Monte Santa Tecla but that I needed to figure out how to get there. I told him that before leaving for the Camino, I'd read that at one time pagan Druids had lived there. Pilgrims who visited the site of the ruins often had some sort of mystical spiritual experience. The stories I'd read intrigued me enough to make this side trip, before going home.

George offered to take me to the bus terminal and the train station to check the schedules. We drove there only to find out I'd just missed the last train. Very quickly, he drove to the bus terminal. George knew the guy working behind the counter. He said there was a bus leaving in forty-five minutes. His friend took my backpack for safe-keeping and we left the station and drove to a café. When we got there George knew everyone and proudly introduced me to all of his friends. He was a gregarious man with a delightful sense of humour. It seemed everyone loved being around him, especially the ladies. He ordered a beer and I had juice and a sandwich, which he insisted on paying for. I began to get anxious about making it to the mountain before nightfall. George suddenly jumped up realizing it was late and I might miss the bus. He assured me he would see to it that I got to Monte Santa Tecla that night, even if he had to drive me there himself. We got in his little car and he drove like a madman to the bus terminal. My bus had just pulled out of the gate when we arrived.

George ran into the station, retrieved my backpack from his friend, threw it into the back seat and hopped back in the car. With one hand on the steering wheel and the other on the gearshift, he sped down the road that ran along the bank of the river Mino. I buckled my seat belt. George didn't. He drove like Steve McQueen tearing past dozens of cars. We finally caught up with the bus and George started honking his horn continuously. The bus driver refused to slow down. Frustrated, George pulled out to pass on the left and gunned it, still honking the horn as he pulled up beside the bus. He called out to the driver in Portuguese and waved his hand out the window, but still no reaction. Finally he zoomed past the bus and pulled directly in front, blocking it. The bus braked to a stop.

Relieved that the chase was over, I thanked George for getting me there safely. He got out and passed me my backpack. I kissed him on each cheek. Patting my back, he wished me a safe journey. The bus doors swung open. I thanked the driver for stopping, paid 1.85 Euros and found a seat at the back. The bus dropped me off at a ferry terminal. While waiting for the ferry I watched four men playing dominos in a café, enjoying their shouts and laughter as they slapped down their tiles. Shortly after, the ferry took us back across the river Mino, to Spain again. I knew we were close to the mouth of the river where it empties into the Atlantic, but I couldn't actually see it. I found an empty seat on a bench on the outside deck where it was extremely windy and freezing cold. I was shocked to see two young girls on a dock straining to carry a double rowing scull being buffeted by the wind. I couldn't believe they would even attempt to row in these conditions without a coach. As the ferry went by, I watched them launch the scull in the waves and quickly feathered the oars. They dropped them into the river and pulled with force, gracefully gliding through the water—in total control. I was impressed. Fortunately, it was only a short boat ride and I arrived on the other side in ten minutes.

I found out it was a two-kilometre walk from there to the mountain. Many cars passed me as I trudged along the shoulder of the road. I saw a truck across the street with an older driver talking to the gas bar attendant. I crossed the street and asked if they spoke English. The gas attendant spoke a little. I told them I was going to Monte Santa Tecla and since I'd already walked twenty-eight kilometres that day, I asked if the driver could he give me a ride. The gas attendant translated my request. Immediately, the trucker pointed to the passenger door. I assumed that meant he would take me so I got in. We drove in silence and in a few minutes, he dropped me off at the town at the base of the mountain. I thanked him and got out of the truck. From there, it was another kilometre walk up a path to the top of the mountain. The sun was setting and I was anxious about getting there while it was still daylight. I stopped a woman on the street and thankfully, she understood English. I asked her if there was a bus that went to the top of the mountain. She shook her head and said it stopped running in the afternoon. She pointed to a taxi stand with a line-up of white taxis waiting. I approached one of the drivers and asked if he could pick me at 9:00 p.m. that night on the mountain. He agreed.

33

Celtic Connection

There were no yellow or blue arrows marking the trail up Monte Santa Tecla. Instead, there was a path that led me to Christian stone crosses that guided the way to the Druidic ruins. Each cross depicted one of the fourteen stages of the Passion of Jesus carrying the cross before his death. I picked up stones along the way and ritualistically placed one on the ground at each station.

At the top of the mountain, I leaned out over the edge. It was a sheer drop of at least five hundred metres to the water below. There was no safety barrier, and although afraid of heights, I was drawn to watch the wild, crashing waves below. Taking stock, I felt physically exhausted yet spiritually, I was calm and at peace with myself. Even so, I was in a strange mood. Having completely surrendered to the idea of returning home with the Eagle Feather, I no longer felt any pressure or fear.

A path meandered past a tourist bar, souvenir shops and restaurant. I went in to buy a drink and found everything was closing down for the night. After buying some juice, I began walking cautiously down another rocky path on the other side of the mountain. Coming to an ancient ruin, I entered what remained of the stone structure. The wind howled mournfully. Sadly, graffiti had been sprayed on the broken stone walls and there was litter all around. I picked up some of the trash and stuffed as much as I could into my pockets.

Walking around the ruins, I placed my bare hands on the cold stones. They felt alive. Since I had learned to put my sorrow into stones, I was aware of the strong connection I had to them and the stories they held. Optimistically, I put my ear up against a wall and listened for the voices of my Celtic ancestral spirits, but nothing came through. I stood in silence, holding a sacred space in honour of them. The sun began to set casting a beam of light through an open door frame, projecting my long pilgrim shadow across the uneven stone floor. I walked around and continued to pick up garbage, saddened by the broken glass littered on the uneven stone floor.

I left the building and climbing further down the path, I came across a promontory jutting out from the mountain. It was covered in a series of concentric and side-by-side circles made with blocks of stones that looked like the foundations for the round Celtic houses known as *palloza's*. There were some small bushes and overgrown grass growing around the circular structures. Intrigued, I walked toward one of the larger circles and climbed over the stone wall that stood about knee-high. Once inside the first circle, I slipped off my pack and sat on the ground cross-legged in the centre. I closed my eyes and began to breathe with focussed awareness, moving into a meditative state. My mind calmed quickly as I eased into the moment.

Facing west with my eyes closed, I felt the warm light from the setting sun caressing me while the distinct sound of the waves crashing on rocks far below kept me in an alert state. The cool wind wrapped around my body and ran across my lips. The gentle movement of the air around me, added to the aura of this mystical place. Sitting with my base chakra connected to the ground, I was still. Open to receiving all the love of the universe, time passed without my awareness of its passing. My body was charged. Slowly, I opened my eyes. I was even more sensitive to my physical surroundings; the colors of the sky, the texture of the ground, the shapes of the stone structures and the movement of the wind. All of these were incredibly vivid, sharply etched in my mind. I stood and gathered up my pack. I walked out of the stone circle and continued my descent following a path down the mountainside.

I was startled by an abrupt movement further along in the bushes. A beautiful white dog appeared. It started to walk toward one of the stone circles when, suddenly, it stopped and turned its head. Holding its sleek muscular body perfectly still, the dog looked directly into my eyes. Neither of us moved. I was stunned by the absolute beauty of this animal. I wanted to move closer but without warning, the dog swiftly turned around and was gone out of sight. It was a surreal moment. I wasn't sure if the white dog had actually been there, or had I just imagined it?

It was dusk now and the stars were beginning to appear in the twilight sky above. Since there was no one else on the mountain, it created the perfect environment from me to go into an altered state. The circle in front of me was completely enclosed with other stone circles that linked to its exterior wall creating a geometric pattern. I felt called to it. I took off my pack and left it outside the circle. I climbed over the wall, placing my hand on the ancient stones for support. Entering the second stone circle, I immediately resonated with a spiritual energy I felt there. Quietly sitting cross-legged on the cool earth, my mind stilled. Initially, I felt its dampness and started to shiver. Then after taking several long, deep breaths, a sense of warmth and lightness overcame me, and a tingling sensation rushed throughout my body as if each cell was vibrating at a higher frequency. Hearing the fluid motion of the water below I began moving my body along with it's rhythm. Closing my eyes, I followed my breath, going deeper and slower. I drew on the kundalini energy pulling it up through the chakras with my breath, to awaken my consciousness. I felt the reddened heat of a primordial fire race throughout me.

In the quiet of my centered mind, I heard the faint sound of women's voices playfully laughing and singing behind me. I had to sit very still to hear them, any movement or sound seemed to disturb their presence. Bagpipes and medieval instruments were playing Celtic music. In the distance, there was the rhythmic tap of a tambourine playing. With my eyes closed, there was the sensation that a group of women had entered the space. They came in one by one. I wondered if they knew I was there. I couldn't see them at first, but their presence was confirmed with a gentle brush across my cheek; like the kiss I received from the man in my dream. I wondered if they were telling me that everything would be alright, too. I was filled with anticipation.

I kept my eyes closed, smiling amicably as they made themselves known. They danced around me clock-wise, each woman acknowledging me as she came into view and then floated out of sight behind me. A continuous low drone sound filled the entire circle. There was giggling and laughter as they playfully danced in front of me. Their voices moved around the circle, growing in volume as they gathered harmonic momentum. Their bodies flowed gracefully, like the amniotic waves in a mother's womb. They danced barefoot around the inside of the stone walls, clad in flowing long dresses. Without effort I began to sway to the music, rocking from side to side, their dance inviting me in. A young woman played a miniature harp, others played flutes. An older gray-haired woman played a small stringed instrument like a mandolin, while her sisters sang along in celebration of the feminine spirit. There was a knowing I was accepted as a part of their sisterhood.

Suspended in the moment, I felt a gentle shifting of the earth beneath me. The dancing women had slipped a yellow silk carpet under me and celebrated my acceptance by lifting me up into the air. The carpet held my weight easily and by taking turns holding it, they raised me up and then lowered me down as if we were drifting on a slow moving merry-go-round. Their playful medieval music increased the intensity of the ancestral ceremony. The constant circular movement had made me dizzy. I felt nauseous and a little queasy. For a split second I became afraid and considered leaving the space. With that thought, it was over in an instant. The music stopped and the women floated away disappearing into the darkness. I wanted to call them back but something told me my thought had broken the spell. Not sure what to expect, I slowly opened my eyes. Nothing had changed. I was still sitting cross-legged on the ground in the middle of a stone circle. Night had fallen and I was shivering from the cold. I stood up, gathered my backpack and started to walk again, stepping in and out of the stone circles. The soft moonlight lit the path to guide me down the steep descent. A horn honked. I looked up to see a white car. My taxi had arrived.

34

A Dusty Moment

The plane roared down the runway and climbed into the air. Once it levelled out, I relaxed into my seat, closed my eyes and reminisced about the journey. I had to confess, I was surprised at how much I had learned on this pilgrimage. It was a completely different approach to peregrination than I had ever imagined. I had suffered with blisters on my feet, stones trapped under my skin and getting lost many times. By walking in both directions like the pilgrims of the past, I had stepped into their footsteps and had seen my journey from a completely different perspective. I had experienced humility, losing my eyeglasses, asking for food, sleeping on a gym floor and being mugged. I enjoyed the unconditional love, kindness and the honour of being served by strangers along the way. But more importantly, on this path I was carrying the sacred Native Eagle Feather on its life journey.

Nearing my destination, I thought about the next step of my journey. I'd arranged to meet Andreas during my stopover in Frankfurt and spend some time with him. The excitement of seeing him so soon after walking the Camino was unbearable. I twirled my hair around my index finger until it was tightly knotted and I couldn't get my finger out. Eventually we touched down in Germany. Disembarking the plane was a slow process, made slower by my anxiousness to see Andreas again. Through the crowds in the arrivals area I caught a glimpse of him. He smiled, characteristically bending his head to the side. Time slowed down as I moved closer to him and I lost the sense of where I was.

"Hello pilgrim," he said, repeating the greeting we had used all the time on the phone. I dropped my bag on the floor and wrapped my arms around him. He held me close. I was struck by the familiar scent of his skin. He put his hand on the back of my head pulling me closer to him, the side of my face resting close to his heart. I listened to his breath and then lifted my head up to meet his eyes.

"Andreas," I whispered, "I've missed you so much." Our lips touched and we kissed. A surge of loving energy rushed through my body. I couldn't move. The profound intensity of our absolute love was ever-present. Spiritually reconnected, we returned to the familiar rhythm of our simple pilgrim world. We stood there bathed in the aura of each other's presence for what seemed like hours. Nothing needed to be said.

"Come on, Sue, let's go," he said breaking the silence. "I want to show you the romantic Rhine Valley." He took my backpack, slid it over his shoulder and we walked arm in arm to his car. He had a beard now and his dark hair was impeccably styled. Wearing a red wool sweater and pressed jeans, he looked different than the pilgrim I remembered. He had a rental car, a stunning new navy blue 2004 BMW 5 Series; something I would have desired prior to walking the Camino. Andreas gallantly opened my door and I jumped in. We traveled along the Rhine admiring the vineyards and breathtaking countryside. The sky was a perfect soft blue with puffy low-hanging clouds everwhere.

Andreas had suggested we stop in a small village to taste the famous *kaffee* served in this region. We noticed crowds of people going into a church. A sign publicized that there was a concert starting at 5:30 p.m.—in just a few minutes. A choir and an orchestra would be performing Bach, Strauss and Handel. It was perfect timing so we went in and walked up to the front. The church was filled with statues of saints painted in soft shades of blue, yellow, rose pink and green. From the high nave, tiny lights were suspended just above our heads. The altar was in the Baroque style, very ornate with gold trim everywhere. We took a seat just as the concert started. After being in the comfort and silence of Mother Nature for nineteen days, listening to the classical music was so emotional, it moved me to tears.

We left after the concert was finished and drove along the Rhine valley to another small village where we stopped for Italian gelato at an outdoor café. Andreas wanted to hear all about my Camino, so I did most of the talking. We were about to leave as he pointed out a beautiful medieval castle perched on top of a mountain. He said it was now a famous hotel called Eltz Castle. It looked like something out of a fairy tale.

"It's very romantic," I said in awe of its grandeur.

"Let's stay there tonight," he suggested looking at me with his eyebrows raised in anticipation of my response. With some hesitation I agreed, well aware that spending the night together in a castle could make it more difficult not to fall in love with him again. We drove across bridge and up a steep road that wound along the edge of the forested mountainside. We parked the car and walked over a stone crossing above the moat that surrounded the medieval hotel. Andreas checked-in while I wandered around the lobby admiring the antique furniture and paintings. He returned with a key and a porter who gladly carried my soiled backpack to our room.

It was huge and overlooked the grounds of the twelfth century palace. The bed had a sheer canopy that hung loosely over the wooden frame; at least a dozen pillows covered the fluffy white cotton duvet. It was excessive, and not just by pilgrim standards. As it was getting late and we were starving, we just dropped our things and hurried back downstairs to the dining room before it closed. The formal restaurant was elegantly decorated and filled with fine antiques. Dressed in my pilgrim clothes, I felt out of place. The waiter was efficient and provided very formal service. Andreas reviewed the menu with me and then ordered for both of us. We sat by a window overlooking the last moments of the gorgeous view as darkness set around us. We eased into a familiar conversation as though we had known each other for several lifetimes. Being there with Andreas felt as though I had been re-united with a very dear old friend. Andreas leaned over and took my hand in his.

"I think I'm falling in love with you again, Sue Kenney," he said lovingly. A feeling of absolute love vibrated in every cell of my body. I looked away and then back into his eyes pleading with him not to go there. We finished our meal and went back to the room. Thrilled not to be in a bunk, I jumped on the enormous bed just like I did the first night we stayed together at the Parador Hotel in Santiago. I was giggling a lot, partly because of excitement but mostly because I was nervous about how the night would unfold. I had a relaxing bath and changed into my only clean clothes; a T-shirt and black sports underwear. I slipped into the fluffy white bathrobe that I found hanging on the back of the bathroom door. I wrapped it tightly around me. Andreas was already sitting in bed reading when I came out of the bathroom.

As pilgrims on the Camino, we had made an agreement that we would always try to live in the moment, without expectation of the outcome. We trusted and believed that the Camino would guide us, both on the pilgrim path and on our life journey. Looking across the room at him, I knew for sure that there was no way that I was going to fall romantically in love again. We had already been down that path and it would be too easy to go back to where we left off. Besides, with the Eagle Feather still in my possession, I felt an obligation to complete my quest without the distraction of romance. Feeling confident about my decision, I quickly slid under the heavy comforter and sat up beside him. Taking my hand, Andreas leaned in closer and told me that he would honour my request not to fall in love again. There was a long silent pause. I moved my tongue to the corner of my mouth, tasting a salty tear that had rolled down the side of my face. With a gentle touch, Andreas wiped it away.

"Sue, I give you all of the love of the universe." All of a sudden, there was a spark of love that ignited a warm golden sensation in my heart and then moved to every cell in my body. I was reminded of the moment on Cebreiro when I had sent all the love of the universe to Andreas. Like a mirror he sent it back to me. He'd said that it wasn't his to keep. That night we'd connected to the place of absolute love, but this time it was Andreas who was giving me all of the love of the universe and it was my turn to decide whether to keep it or not.

"Andreas," I said lovingly. "This love is not mine to keep." With those words, I reflected all the love back to him and he accepted it. I knew for certain that ours was an eternal love with no beginning and no end. This miraculous moment marked completion of yet another circle.

The next day we walked along the Rhine enjoying the summer-like temperatures and the last few moments of each other's company. Andreas was going back home to Berlin and had booked a flight close to my departure time. We took the rental car back to the airport, checked in and got our boarding passes. We went to an exclusive lounge for frequent flyers. Andreas was a member because his work as an international consultant required him to travel often.

The lounge was almost full and we had difficulty finding two seats where we could sit together. We sat down and almost right away Andreas left to use the washroom.

Knowing that I had a long flight home, I looked over the complimentary food table and spied an oval tray piled high with enormous shortbread cookies. Unable to resist, I took two. The shortbread was so light that when I took a bite the entire thing fell apart in my mouth and hands. Cookie crumbs and powdered sugar landed on the front of my black top, nicely outlining the shape of my breasts. Embarrassed, I looked around to see if anyone was watching. Andreas had seen the entire episode and was laughing. I tried to brush it off but I seemed to be making even more of a mess. He sat down beside me and I offered him the other cookie. He took a bite and the same thing happened to him. Now we were both laughing.

"Look at me," he said, "I'm all dusty."

I froze. "Dusty?" I blurted out. I couldn't believe I'd finally heard that word. I helped him brush off his red sweater while trying to comprehend what was happening in that moment. "Andreas, you know I'm carrying a sacred Eagle Feather that was given to me by my friend Sherry who had a vision in a dream," I said.

"Yes, I remember you telling me. Can I see it?" he asked. I ritualistically unzipped the pouch and took it out. I un-wrapped the bright red fabric and held the Eagle Feather in my hands. Then I offered it to him to hold.

"It's beautiful, isn't it?" I said proudly. I spoke more slowly, "In the dream, she was told to send me on a mission to find someone to carry the Eagle Feather and the message of her people." I explained how the story of the Eagle Feather was based on what has been orally passed on by the First Nation people for over 5000 years and that the Eagle had volunteered to carry messages from the people to the Creator. "And she also told me that the recipient would acknowledge me with love, honour and kindness."

"What are you going to do with it now?" He asked with genuine concern, handing the Eagle Feather back to me.

"I'm not sure but I know one thing for certain, it's not mine to keep," I said confidently. "I'm only the messenger." I looked at Andreas who was captivated by the story and continued speaking. "Sherry also said in the dream that she was told I would give it to someone who was not from Canada." Looking down at my sweater,

I said, "She also told me it would be dusty when I met them." He smiled at me and looked down at his sweater too.

"Why don't you give it to me, Sue?" He said calmly. "I'll take good care of it and share the message of Sherry's people." Ecstatic by his obvious self-selection, I considered his offer. He was a pilgrim and a great storyteller too. Since I first met him he had acknowledged me with, love, honour and kindness. On the Camino, when I gave him all the love of the universe on Cebreiro, he didn't keep it and because of that, I was sure that he wouldn't keep the Eagle Feather either. It was Andreas who had told me the story of the Sorrow Stones. At that time he had made it very clear that he didn't actually believe in the power of the stones. He said it was just a story that he was sharing with me.

"Andreas, do you believe in the story of the Eagle Feather?" It was important for me to know that he truly believed in the story. I waited with anticipation for his response.

"Yes, Sue. I believe in the story," he said confidently.

"Pilgrim, take this Eagle Feather with you on your life journey. As you travel, you will go to a country that you are not from, and there, you will give it to someone who is not from your country." He graciously took the Eagle Feather and continued to listen closely to my words while caressing it. I told him how to pray in the morning facing the east, just as the sun was rising, and to begin each prayer with the words *Miigwech Creator*. He placed the Eagle Feather in the red cloth and carefully folded the corners. I explained how it must be properly cared for and never exposed to alcohol or mood altering drugs. He nodded in agreement and wrapped it up, pulling the deerskin ties tightly. I was confident that he understood his mission.

Over the loudspeaker, the announcer made the final call for Andreas' flight back to Berlin. We both stood up and embraced for a long time. He picked up his bag and as he walked to the gate I thought about how much this story was like the moral of the fable of the Sorrow Stones. It was my total unwavering belief in Sherry's dream that sent me on a life-altering journey with the sacred Eagle Feather. It would be Andreas' belief in the Eagle Feather that would carry the legend of the Native people all over the world. In the end, what I thought I knew was not that important. It's what I believed that really mattered.

On the Camino Andreas had told me the Sorrow Stone story and he had given all the love back to me so I could go on to live my life purpose. On this journey, I had told him the Eagle Feather story and returned all of the love back to him. Maybe this would open the possibility that he could live his life purpose too.

Another circle was complete.

35

Black Ice

Since the book about my first journey, *My Camino*, was now published and the Eagle Feather safely delivered to a worthy recipient, I was finally free to pursue my romantic relationship with Bruce. When I got home from the Camino, he was waiting for me and we fell in love. We spent all of our time together and funnily enough, we even entered a three-day novel writing contest in Muskoka, co-writing a romantic comedy about a woman author and her editor.

Almost a year had passed since I walked both directions of the Portuguese Route of the Camino de Santiago de Compostela. Again, my storytelling vocation called to me. It was time to write the book you are reading now. Feeling the need to be alone to complete my work, I informed Bruce that I had to go away but this time, not to the Camino. Again, he encouraged me to listen to what I was being called to do and do it. Searching the internet I discovered an artists' lodge on the Toronto Islands. In the winter of 2005, I went to Gibraltar Point Centre for the Arts on Hanlan's Point to write. This is the place where the famous world champion rower, Ned Hanlan, lived and trained. It was an honour for me to be there. I was told that at one time the islands were Native healing grounds, so I thought it would be a perfect place to write this story.

February 2nd, 2005—Groundhog Day.

It's 6:06 a.m. and still dark outside. Everyone else at the lodge is still asleep. It's freezing cold and windy outside. I decide to skip working on my second book, *Confessions of a Pilgrim*, to go skating on Lake Ontario. I strip off my flannel pyjamas and begin dressing in layers. I stuff a warm black furry hat, an extra pair of socks and my favourite hockey skates into the wicker basket mounted on the handlebars of my bicycle. With caution, I pedal over the light dusting of snow covering the frozen path.

The frigid air creeps up the sleeves of my coat. It slips under my fleece jacket. The biting wind hits my eyeballs and it feels like they momentarily freeze. Tears trickle down my face. I am smiling with my mouth closed because my teeth are sensitive to the cold. My head is bent down, cutting into the wind. I ride past the new Island School and follow the winding path eastward. My thighs burn as I pedal faster and faster. Breathing freezing air into my lungs forces them to tighten up. My head aches from the cold.

The faster I pedal, the colder it gets. The colder it gets, the faster I pedal. It's a vicious bicycle. I smile at my own atrocious pun. Finding a comfortable pace, I relax my shoulders and tension immediately releases from my body. Following the shore of the lagoon, I pass the Fire Station, the Canoe Club and the bridge to Algonquin Island. I pass The Rectory and still, I haven't seen anyone. I am all alone. It's now light enough to see across the lake to the Toronto city skyline dimly lit. At the Ward's Island ferry docks, I make a sharp turn to the right and follow the snowy path past the ice-rink toward the beach. Once there, I'm unable to push my bike through snow so I stop and set it down. I walk over to the beach. Now shivering from the wind, I sit down on a snow bank and lace up my skates. An older man with a hockey stick skates by. He stops to talk and introduces himself as Jimmy Jones. He's lived on the island all his life, and isn't shy about telling me he'll be seventy-five years this summer.

"In my lifetime, I've never seen the lake like this. It's unusual to see black ice," he said pointing out to the lake. "It never freezes all the way to the Leslie Street Spit on the mainland like it has this year. Who knows how long it will last? I'm skating out there now," he said and invited me to skate to the other side with him. I look out and estimate it is at least two kilometres to the Spit, maybe farther. I know it's dangerous to skate on the thin ice, especially on Lake Ontario. I'm deathly afraid of water yet, strangely, I've been drawn to it all my life. I'm even an excellent swimmer, rower and boater. Standing there in the bay, I'm scared of breaking through and drowning in the freezing water but I don't want to pass up the opportunity to live in the moment. It's a once in a lifetime chance to be on this lake while it stands still, literally frozen in time. So, I decide to trust in the stranger and take a chance.

Leaving the safety of the shore, I hear the sound of ice cracking. Spider cracks run beneath my skates. I can see clearly that the ice is only a few inches thick. It's crystal clear and my eyes see something resting on the bottom of the lake. It's a plastic grocery bag waving back and forth in the current. I watch it, mesmerized by the graceful movement of a piece of garbage. Jimmy calls for me to join him. I skate nervously over the cracks, no longer able see the bottom.

A sudden loud popping noise comes from the ice. I stop skating. Danger is imminent and all my senses are on high alert. My heart beats loudly. It occurs that I am being tested in some way and I'm suddenly frozen with fear. I face danger if I go forward and danger if I go back. Then I remember what I had learned on the Camino—just put one foot in front of the other. As long as I keep moving I will go somewhere. I take a step and then glide. I take another step and before I know it the movement is automatic. I'm skating faster. With each step I'm also getting closer to being out of my comfort zone.

We are in the middle of a vast open plain of wind, ice and snow. I bump over pressure ridges and freshly sealed cracks, my skates rocking up and down throwing me off balance. I can see the ice isn't very thick. I spot a huge sheet of ice suspended below the surface. By shifting the weight of my body, it shifts up and down. I'm on the verge of calling out to Jimmy for help. Frigid Lake Ontario water forces its way through tiny cracks, and I want to cry. I know it won't take much weight to break through, both literally and figuratively. I skate closer to Jimmy.

The clouds slip away and bright sun warms my face. The ice surface is becoming wet and shiny. I'm worried that it will melt before we make it back. I consciously cast myself farther into the unknown, skating as fast as I can over the weakest points. I don't want to end up like the mythical Icarus who flew too close to the sun and the wax holding his feather wings together melted from the heat, sealing his doom. The Spit is closer and now I can see the rocky edge, trees along the shore and a red and white lighthouse on the point. A bevy of white swans swim in open water about twenty metres from where I'm skating. They stop swimming, seeming to watch me. Just as I approach the mainland, a loud thunderous crack rips across the ice and I leap off the frozen water falling safely into the snow on the shore.

"*Miigwech Creator,*" I said with great relief as I look around. Then Jimmy skates up to me. I stand up and turn to see where I have come from. Having reached the half-way point, I know I must skate back across the ice to the place where I started.

36

The Pilgrim Way

Having a book published was one thing, but once it was out, I was resistant to traditional marketing. Remembering that the stories from the Camino were a gift and that I had an obligation to share with others, I knew that if I shared my story from a place of love, I could open the possibility for people to self-select to read the book or not. First I had to let them know that it existed. So, I travelled all over Canada telling stories at book signings, doing author readings, writing articles, doing storytelling festivals, conferences and media interviews. I personally handed out more than 70,000 promotional bookmarks leaving them everywhere I went. I've told the Sorrow Stone story on countless occasions and have given away thousands of stones as well.

One day, I was invited to do a live interview on Breakfast Television in Halifax to talk about *My Camino*. Just before leaving, I contacted the manager of the local Coles Books Store to ask if I could do a book signing while I was in the city. Kara, the store manager was very flexible and agreed to my visit, even though there wasn't time to promote the event. After the television interview, I arrived at the mall early. I met Kara, an energetic enthusiastic young woman. She was thrilled to have me do a book signing and had already set up a table at the door.

Quickly, I set up my display. Positioning a stack of bookmarks at either end of the table, I placed my books and storytelling CD in the in the centre. Then I put a bowl filled with polished stones beside them with a sign that said, "Free Stones. Please Take One." People immediately gathered around, curious about who I was and why I was giving away stones. Within five minutes there was a large group standing around the table listening to my story of the Sorrow Stones.

While I spoke, an older couple stopped and stood away from the crowd, off to one side. The man was exceptionally tall with thick gray hair. His petite wife stood with her hands in her pockets, watching me closely as I told the story. On the Camino, I'd learned not to judge people by their reactions or make assumptions about who I thought needed to hear its message. As a messenger, I was sharing a simple story that had been shared with me. Through my journey, I had learned to remain open to the possibility that people would self-select how much they wanted to believe, if any of it at all. When I finished, the couple who had stopped, came forward and thanked me for telling them the story of the Sorrow Stones. I offered them a stone. The man informed me that they find stones everywhere they go and feel compelled to bring them home. He spoke with pride about their son who had studied to be geologist and also loved stones.

"Would you like to take a stone for your son?" I suggested pointing at the bowl. The couple exchanged a look and the woman turned her head away.

"Our son was killed in a diving accident," the man said, "it happened just off the coast of Newfoundland while doing research on scallop shells." I paused, waiting for him to continue. Since their son's death, he told me, they'd been collecting stones but they weren't sure why. They believed that in some way the stones would help them overcome their sorrow and loss. They explained that was why they were so moved by my story. The man reached into his pocket and took something out. He opened the palm of his hand so

I could see there was a silver pendant about the size of quarter in the shape of a scallop shell. It was so worn that the lines of the shell were barely visible and it was now shiny and smooth. "It was our son's," he said proudly.

"So your son was a pilgrim," I added with excitement. They looked at each other somewhat confused. I told them the story of how pilgrims of the past would pick up a scallop shell from the ocean in Fisterra and take it home as proof they had walked the Camino. I explained how it has become the international symbol of a pilgrim. The scallop shell pendant he showed me was a clear message that their son was a pilgrim in life, even though he had never walked the Camino. The father looked at the mother and then picked up one of my books.

"We'd like to buy your book. Would you sign it for us please?" the mother said. Thrilled at their request, I picked up my treasured fountain pen, the one I use for signing books, and asked them what name I should dedicate it to. They answered in unison. "Allen."

I looked up from the book. "Is that your son's name?" I asked.

"Yes," the woman responded, her voice breaking. Looking down at the book, I realized this was a very precious request. With earnest, I put my intention into the fountain pen as I wrote the words:

To Allen,
From one pilgrim to another. May you find eternal peace on your journey along the way.
Buen Camino.
Sue Kenney
2005

I gently closed the book, pausing for a moment in a state of absolute gratitude. With both hands, I presented it to the couple along with my intentions for eternal love. The man opened the book and read the inscription. His wife took my hand and squeezed it tightly. Then she picked up a stone and as they turned to walk away, I noticed she was rubbing it between her fingers. A tingling sensation rushed through my body covering me with goose-bumps. Suddenly, I realized another crowd had gathered around the table and I began telling the Sorrow Stone story once again.

Epilogue

I call myself a pilgrim because I have walked the medieval pilgrimage route called the Camino de Santiago de Compostela in Spain. I believe that we are all pilgrims, each on our own journey to find the way. The Camino is my life and now when I look back at this quest, I realize that perhaps the purpose of being a messenger on the journey of the Eagle Feather was to guide me to continue to live my life purpose.

As I had promised the Creator, I continue to share the story of the Eagle Feather with people all over the world fulfilling my vocation as a messenger by using my voice to inspire others. Almost daily I receive e-mails from people who are inspired by my Camino stories. Many write to ask for my advice and insights into the allure of this mystical path. It's an ongoing process. I believe that by telling the stories of my Camino guides others to apply the lessons of a pilgrimage, as a metaphor for a life journey. At this time, Andreas still has the Eagle Feather in his possession. He continues to honour it and share the story of its journey. Walking the return path of this journey definitely made the integration of this Camino easier for me when I got back home. Although, I've learned before, when the Camino ends the journey just begins.

The book *My Camino* is a national best seller and the movie rights for a feature film adaptation of the book have been secured by the Oscar-nominated Montreal based Cirrus Productions. I firmly believe that by choosing to live my life purpose and extolling the virtues of being a pilgrim, the Camino has provided all these things and opened the potential for me to create unlimited possibilities that I could never have dreamed of before.

I am living a dream I didn't know I had.

Sue Kenney
Pilgrim. Author. Speaker.
Filmmaker.

As a pilgrim, Sue Kenney has walked over 2000 kilometres of the Camino on the French Route, Portuguese Route, English Route, Fisterra Route and Roman/Muxia Route. Sue wrote, produced and recorded a storytelling CD, Stone by Stone and she is a writer. Sue's first book, *My Camino*, was published by White Knight Books and is a Canadian bestseller. It has been optioned by Cirrus Productions in Montreal, Quebec, for a feature film adaptation of the book. *Confessions of a Pilgrim* is her second book.

In 2006 Sue directed her first feature length documentary called *Las Peregrinas ... the women who walk*. Here she documents the journey of five women who walk a section of the Camino with in October 2005. She has co-produced another short film based on the book *Confessions of a Pilgrim* with Bookshorts Moving Stories which has been broadcast on television nationally. Sue is also the Producer of a BravoFACT Awarded short animated film called *FlipBook* about the creative process of writing. Sue has written and performs *My Camino* as a one-woman theatrical storytelling performance at the London Fringe Festival and other theatres. Sue also publishes and distributes a monthly newsletter called Inspirational Moments that focuses on the Camino. As a freelance writer she has written for newspapers, magazines, websites and periodicals.

Sue's plans are to keep walking. She continues to live the Camino everyday and her vocation in life by using her voice to tell stories. Sue is presently living near Washago with her partner Bruce Pirrie.

About Sue's Inspirational Speaking, Life Coaching and Workshops

Blended with her profound experiences as a pilgrim, her athletic discipline as a competitive Master's rower and her extensive background in the corporate telecommunications industry, Sue provides leadership coaching, workshops, and inspirational speaking to both community and business audiences. Sue offers a unique perspective to developing personal and principled leadership skills based on the applying the virtues of a pilgrim on the Camino, as a metaphor for a life journey.

Sue shares stories from the journey on the Camino, her background as a world class competitive rower and over 20 years in the corporate telecom industry to impart valuable life lessons to deliver inspiring and entertaining stories of leadership.

As a speaker and life coach Sue Kenney is ...

• Inspirational—a sought after internationally acclaimed speaker and performer who creates a powerful and memorable experience for her audiences that range from 20-500 people.

• Engaging and funny-she tells true stories of inspiration

• A Leader: Opens possibilities through the process of attracting what is earnestly desired.

• Aware of the power of the present moment to guide vision, mission and purpose.

• Able to shift perspective and increase productivity through efficient thinking.

• A National Best Selling Author of her book called *My Camino*

• Creative and visionary leader who coaches principled leadership

• Producer and director of three films in 2006 and continues to inspire others to discover their creative potential.

• Someone who has spoken to over 5000 people on the topic of leadership.

Workshop Topics
Leadership. Creativity. Creating Balance. Choice. Effective Thinking. Being vs Doing. Attraction. Creating Intentions. Breathwork.
For customized speaking, coaching or workshop needs contact us at sue.kenney@sympatico.ca

WWW.SUEKENNEY.CA

Testimonials

"Sue, I have attended many motivational speaker sessions over the last 15 years and felt yours was one of my favorites.... ranking up there with Jim Rohn and Mark Victor Hansen. You delivered a moving, inspirational, heart inspired story of conquering life's fears and living life to its absolute fullest. You painted word pictures so vividly that I could see myself following in the amazing steps of your journey with the same passion you delivered your talk with. Outstanding!"
D'arcie Rogers, CFP, CDS, TEP,
Executive Financial Consultant, Calgary

"Often we are prevented from producing to our full potential because of our fears. Sue Kenney faced many fears in her own life, and was able to overcome them. She is an inspiration and a guide for others."
G. Philip Fisher, Advocis School, Banff

I just heard you on the CBC and was compelled to go to your website. I've read "the Pilgrimage" by Paolo Coelho and was completely taken by his journey, the same one you have made yourself. It was fortuitous that my dial is always tuned to the CBC and you happened to be one of the callers that I listened to. As I've come to understand there is no such thing as a coincidence so I thank you for inspiring me to visit your website—I will certainly purchase your book and just maybe make that walk some time soon. Thank you
Lucy Riolino, Administrative Assistant, Casino Niagara

Hello Sue:
I heard you speak at the Leadership Roundtable Alumni Session at the City of Hamilton. You were fabulous! Your stories & amazing slides of your trip through Spain and your rowing experiences are definitely linked to the theme and it would be great to inspire our group.
Liz Sisolak Employee Wellness Coordinator
Human Resources, City of Hamilton

Hello Sue, I just wanted to mention that I saw you on Breakfast Television last week and you made a tremendous impact using your sorrow stones story. Congratulations on all of your success!
Joyce Paron, EXIT Reality Corp International, Toronto

Sue Kenney is an ex-Bell employee who left Bell to pursue and amazing, life changing journey. Sue's inspirational style is completely motivating and captivating, you won't be disappointed!!!!
Lori Lennox, Bell Canada

Sue, I bought your DVD, book, and CD tonight after hearing your story, and am really looking forward to immersing myself in them. You have inspired me to continue to move forward, literally and figuratively. Anyway, I wanted to express my heartfelt gratitude for the time you spent with us tonight. I believe the Universe brought you into my life for a purpose. Momentary or otherwise, thank-you.
Linda Borland-Fitzgerald, Barrie

My Camino

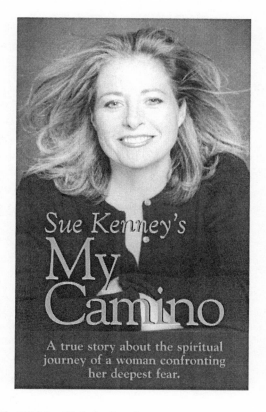

Published by White Knight Books
Book design by Karen Pletherick
Photo courtesy of Yanka and Yolanda Vanderkolk

Sue Kenney's
My Camino
Published by White Knight Books
$19.95

In October 2001, after being suddenly downsized from her position as an account executive with an international telecommunications company Sue Kenney decided to go for a long walk. Five weeks later, she took her first step on the Camino de Santiago de Compostela; a medieval pilgrimage route in Spain. She walked 780 kilometers over 29 days, in the winter and she went alone. The journey was a life altering experience, filled with incredible lessons. On the path Sue realized her purpose was to inspire people using her voice to tell stories.

When she returned home, she began telling stories about her experiences and the people she met on the Camino. She spoke to community groups, libraries, churches, schools, and has been a keynote speaker at special events. *My Camino* rolled off the press in September 2004 and Sue went on tour. Her book is now a national best seller. Books can be purchased at major and independent book stores or ordered on line at www.suekenney.ca

Documentary
Las Peregrinas

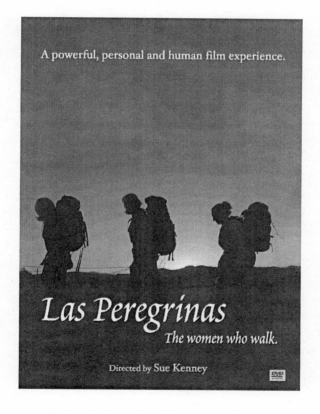

Las Peregrinas ... the women who walk.

Is there something lacking spiritually, emotionally, and physically from the apparently secure and comfortable lives of modern North American women? In this documentary we explore what compelled these and other women to voluntarily choose to suffer both the joys and anguish of walking hundreds, sometimes thousands of kilometers on a medieval pilgrimage route in search of something more.

Sue Kenney, a veteran pilgrim returns to Spain to shepherd a group of first-time women pilgrims (in Spanish known as, Las Peregrinas) on their own individual journeys of self-discovery, where Sue's philosophy and values, as well as the Camino's legendary power to transform lives, will be put to the test.

Las Peregrinas is a powerful and moving documentary about facing our deepest fears by questioning the value of everything that we were taught was important in life.

Directed by Sue Kenney
Produced by Stone by Stone Productions
Locations Spain/Canada Length 85 minutes
Language English/Spanish with English subtitles
To order go to www.suekenney.ca

Spiritual Film Gatherings
If you are interested in sponsoring a screening of Las Peregrinas in your community as a fund raiser or to create an opportunity to gather people together please contact us at www.suekenney.ca

Storytelling CD
Stone by Stone

Stone by Stone…a woman's journey to self-love. A meditative storytelling CD. Sit back and relax as you listen to Sue Kenney telling stories of her journey on the Camino de Santiago de Compostela.

Music by Gary Diggins
Produced and Narrated by Sue Kenney
$15.00 plus taxes
To order copies go to www.suekenney.ca

Reading List and Resources

A Pilgrim's Guide to the Camino Portugues: The Portuguese Way of St. James Porto to Santiago de Compostela by John Brierley

Walking the Camino De Santiago by Bethan Davies and Ben Cole

The Pilgrim's Guide to Santiago De Compostela by William Melczer

All the Good Pilgrims, Tales of the Camino de Santiago by Robert Ward

Among the Pilgrims: Journeys to Santiago de Compostela by Mary Victoria Wallis

A Pilgrim's Guide to the Camino Fisterra: Santiago de Compostela to Finisterre Including the Muxia Extension by John Brierley

Pate, Jam and Good Intentions, Barbara Cappuccitti

Camino Chronicle: Walking to Santiago by Susan Alcorn

The Pilgrimage by Paulo Coelho

What the Psychic Told the Pilgrim: A Midlife Misadventure on Spain's Camino de Santiago by Jane Christmas

El Camino De Santiago: Rites of Passage by Wayne Chimenti

Walking the Via de la Plata: The Camino de Santiago from Sevilla to Santiago de Compostela by Ben Cole and Bethan Davies

El Camino: Walking to Santiago De Compostela (Penn State Series in Lived Religious Experience) by Lee Hoinacki

Fumbling: A Pilgrimage Tale of Love, Grief, and Spiritual Renewal on the Camino de Santiago by Kerry Egan

The Camino: A Journey of the Spirit by Shirley MacLaine

Walking Home on the Camino De Santiago by Linda L. Lasswell

Pilgrim Stories, by Nancy Louise Frey

Pilgrimage to the End of the World: The Road to Santiago de Compostela by Conrad Rudolph

Following the Milky Way: A Pilgrimage on the Camino de Santiago by Elyn Aviva

Travels with My Donkey: One Man and His Ass on a Pilgrimage to Santiago by Tim Moore

Road of Stars to Santiago by Edward F. Stanton

Walk in a Relaxed Manner: Life Lessons from the Camino by Joyce Rupp

Web Sites

www.americanpilgrims.com

www.saintjames@yahoogroups.com

www.santiago.com

www.ultreya.net

www.oakapple.net

www.csj.org.uk

www.gocamino.oakapple.net

www.turgalicia.es

www.caminhodesantiago.com

978-0-595-42790-1
0-595-42790-1